Study Guide

ABNORMAL PSYCHOLOGY
Fifth Edition

Gerald C. Davison
University of Southern California

John Neale
SUNY at Stony Brook

Prepared by

Douglas Hindman
Eastern Kentucky University

WILEY

JOHN WILEY & SONS
New York Chichester Brisbane Toronto Singapore

ISBN 0-471-51857-3
Printed in the United States of America

10 9 8 7 6 5 4 3 2 1

To My Students

This study guide is designed to help you study *Abnormal Psychology: An Experimental Clinical Approach, 5th Edition* by Davison & Neale. Each chapter in this guide provides a number of sections to make your study easier.

Overview sections place the chapter in context by describing it's relationship to the chapters that precede and follow it.

Chapter Summaries, not surprisingly, summarize the chapter.

Study Objectives list the important ideas or concepts in the chapter

Key Terms provide a place for you to write in definitions of technical words introduced in the chapter. Typically these terms are boldfaced in the text.

Study Questions are the questions you should be able to answer from reading each section of the text. The Study Guide provides space for you to write your answers to each question.

Self-Test provides a way for you to check your knowledge of the chapter. The Self-test questions cover the content specified by the Study Questions except for an occasional asterisked (*) test question.

The Study Guide also includes a chapter on *Studying in This Course*. This chapter is based on my experiences helping students improve their study skills. It describes a study method (SQ4R) you can use to improve your study skills. It also provides suggestions for coping with common study problems. I hope you'll find this chapter helpful.

Abnormal psychology is a fascinating, but complex, topic for many students. Hopefully this Study Guide will make your study easier and more profitable. It is based on the experiences, comments and criticisms of hundreds of students who have used it in my classes. I invite you to join them in offering suggestions for further improvements.

Douglas Hindman
Richmond, Kentucky

CONTENTS

Studying in this course
(AND IN OTHER COURSES TOO)

I'm convinced, though it might be hard to prove, that few students get bad grades because they're dumb. There is little in the average college curriculum (including abnormal psychology) that's beyond the intellectual capacities of most college students. I'm convinced most students get poor grades because they don't know how to study.

Being a student is a job. The hours are long and the pay is non-existent but it's still a job. The payoff is the knowledge you gain and the grades you get. You've been at this "job" for many years, and you're probably not through with it. If this is to be your job you might consider how to become good at it. Are you learning? Are you working efficiently and getting the results you should get?

This study guide incorporates features to help you develop good study skills. If you will spend a little time consciously working on your study skills, you can help the process along.

This chapter is intended to help you review and improve your study skills. The first part of the chapter describes a system, SQ4R, you can use in this, or almost any, course. The second part of the chapter contains suggestions for dealing with common study problems.

THE SQ4R STUDY SYSTEM

As you begin to study a new chapter, follow this plan.

SURVEY

First, survey the entire chapter briefly. Take five to ten minutes to get a general idea of the material. Look over the titles and pictures, read the overview, chapter summary, and essential concepts of this study guide and the introduction and summary in the text. While doing this, actively ask yourself what you will be studying. Figure out how the text is organized to cover the topic. Don't read the chapter in detail yet. This brief survey will help you focus your attention and familiarize you with new vocabulary and concepts. Research suggests that surveying the chapter can reduce your study time by 40%.

READ

Read the chapter actively. To read actively, take the first portion of the chapter and turn the main heading or topic into a question. What are you being told? The study questions in this study guide will help you formulate the question.

Then read the first portion, looking for the answer to your question. It is important that you actively seek the answer as you read. Deliberately try <u>not</u> to to read every word. Instead, read for answers.

Typically a text will make several points regarding each general topic. Look for words indicating these points such as, "first", "furthermore", or "finally". Generally a paragraph contains one idea. Additional paragraphs may elaborate on or illustrate the point. You may find it helpful to number each point in the text as you come to it.

WRITE

Write down the answer in your guide. In other courses, take study notes. This step is important. By writing the answer you confirm that you actually understand it. Occasionally you will discover you don't really understand the idea when you try to write it down. That's fine. Go back an read some more until you figure it out.

As you write the answer, strive to use as few words as possible. Being concise is important. Try to come up with a few key words that convey the idea. When you can condense a long portion of text into a few key words that express the whole idea, you know you understand the idea clearly. The few key words you write down will be meaningful to you so you will remember them. Do not write complete sentences or elaborate excessively. The fewer words you can use, the better you probably understand and will remember the concept.

When you finish, go on to read the next portion, write your answer, and repeat until you finish the chapter.

RECITE

After you finish the chapter. Go back and quiz yourself. Do this aloud. Actively speaking and listening to yourself will help you remember.

Look at each question and try to repeat the answer without looking. Cover your answers with a sheet of paper so you don't peek accidently. If you've done the earlier steps well, this won't take much time.

REVIEW

Set aside a few minutes every week to recite the material again. Put several questions together and try to recite all the answers to a whole general topic. If you do this regularly, you'll find it takes little time to refresh yourself for an exam.

Get with a classmate to quiz each other, or ask a friend to read the questions and tell you if your answers make sense. This step helps you understand (not just memorize) the material. As you discuss answers with someone else, you develop new ways of looking at the material. This can be especially helpful when the test questions aren't phrased quite the way you expected.

This technique is one variation of a study method called "SQ4R" (Survey, Question, Read, Rite, Recite, Review). If you're not used to it, it may seem a bit complicated at first. If you check around, though, you will find that the "good" students are already using it or a similar system. Research suggests that SQ4R works. It takes a bit of extra effort to get used to, but remember that studying is a skill and that learning any skill (like typing, driving and playing ball) takes time and practice. You will find, though, that your efforts will pay off in this and in your other courses.

COPING WITH STUDY PROBLEMS

The previous section of this chapter described an active study technique that has proven useful to many students. This section talks about common study complaints and what to do about them.

FINDING THE TIME

Does it seem like you never have time to study - or that you study all the time and still aren't getting results?   Admittedly, study takes time, but let's look at the matter.

The traditional rule of thumb is that you should study two hours outside class for every hour in class.   If that sounds like a lot, consider.   The average college student class load is 15 semester hours. If you study two hours for each class hour that's 30 additional hours for a "work week" of 45 hours.

If you have trouble finding that 45 hours, it's time to look at how you spend your time.   Make a "time log".   You can copy the time log at the end of this chapter or make one of your own.   Use it to record how you spend your time for a week or so.   Don't try to change what you're doing. Just record it.

After a week or so, stop and look at how you're using your time?   There are 90 hours between 8 AM and 11 PM in a six day week.   If you devote half those hours to the "job" of being a student, you'll have 45 hours left.   It's your time.

You may want to schedule your time differently.   You'll need to decide what works for your style and situation.   If you set up a schedule, be sure to include time for things you really enjoy as well as time to eat, do your laundry, etc.

Schedule adequate study time and actually spend it studying.   If you get everything done and have time left over, use it to get ahead in some class.   When your study time is over, you should be able to enjoy other activities without worrying about your "job".

GETTING STARTED

Do you find it difficult to actually get down to work when it's study time?   Many students find it helpful to find or make a specific study place.   It could be a desk in your room, the library, or any place where you won't be disturbed and have access to your books and materials.

Use your study place only to study.   If it has to be a place where you do other things, change it in some way when you use it to study.   For example, if you use the kitchen table, clear it off and place a study light on it before you start to study. If you're interrupted, leave your study place until the interruption is over and you can return to studying.

If you do this, you'll soon get into the habit of doing nothing but studying in your study place and will be able to get to work as soon as you sit down.

READING THE MATERIAL

Some students think that effective study means to "read the chapter" three or four times. This could be called the "osmosis approach" to studying. You expose yourself to the words in the text and hope something will sink in - like getting a sun tan. This approach does not work.

If you just "read the chapter" you'll often realize you've been looking at words but have no idea what they mean. If you come to a difficult idea, you're likely to skip over it. When you re-read the chapter, you're likely to recall that the idea was difficult and skip over it again. The result is that you end up having read the chapter three or four times without understanding most of it.

Instead, use an active study technique like the SQ4R system described earlier. Research indicates that active study techniques can dramatically increase how fast you learn material and how much of it you recall.

UNDERLINING THE TEXT

Many students underline or highlight their texts and it works well - sometimes. For most people underlining is not as efficient as taking notes. The danger in underlining is that you tend to underline things to be learned later rather than learning them now. Thus, you can end up with half the chapter underlined and none of it learned. If you must underline, try to underline as few words as possible in the same way as the "key words" approach described in the "Write" section above. Avoid used textbooks that someone else underlined. They may have been a poor underliner. More importantly, the value of underlining (like the value of taking notes) is in doing it yourself and in learning what's important in the process.

READING SPEED

Are you a slow reader? Slow reading can lead to a number of problems. Most obviously, it takes too long to get through the material. More importantly, you lose interest before you get to the main point. You forget the first part of an idea before you get to the end. (You "lose the forest for the trees.") You may not understand a concept unless it's clearly stated in one sentence. You may misinterpret material because you take so long getting through it that you start reading in your own ideas.

If the description above sounds familiar, you might want to check your reading speed. To check your speed, have someone time you while you read for exactly five minutes. Estimate the total words you've read and divide by five.

To estimate the total words you read; count the number of words in five lines and divide by five to get the average number of words per line. Then count the number of lines you read and multiply by the number of words per line.

For textbook material, an efficient reading speed is about 350 to 400 words per minute--depending on the difficulty of the topic and your familiarity with it. For novels and other leisure reading, many students can read 600 to 800 words per minute and "speed readers" can read much faster. Remember that understanding and flexibility in your reading style is more important than mere speed. But, often, increased speed actually improves your understanding.

You can increase your reading speed to some extent by conscious effort. If you watch someone read, you'll notice that their eyes move in "jerks" across the line. Our eyes can read words only when stopped; we read a group of words, then move our eyes, read the next group of words, and so on. To increase reading speed try to take in more words with each eye stop. Don't be concerned with every "and" or "but." Try to notice only the words that carry the meaning. Read for ideas, not words.

If you read very slowly, you should consider seeking special help. Most campuses now have reading laboratories where you can get specialized instruction and help in increasing your reading speed. Ask your instructor if your school offers such help.

ANALYZING TESTS

Perhaps you studied hard but still did poorly on the test. How can you make sure the same thing doesn't happen again?

You'll find it helpful to analyze what went wrong on each question you missed. You may be able to do this in class or you may need to see your instructor individually.

Take the test and your study notes or study guide. Look at each question you got wrong and reconstruct what happened. Did you have the answer in your notes? If so, why didn't you recognize it on the test? Do this for each question you got wrong and look for a pattern. Here are some possibilities.

Was the answer not in your study notes at all? Perhaps your study notes are incomplete. If they didn't cover all the chapter, then you didn't study everything. Make sure your notes are complete next time.

If your study notes seem complete, go back and compare them to the text. Perhaps you misread the text, got the concept wrong, or only got part of it. Make sure you read the entire section of the text. Sometimes the first sentence of a paragraph only seems to convey the idea. Perhaps, also, you need to read faster. Slow readers often have trouble with complex concepts that aren't clearly stated in one sentence.

Perhaps your study notes didn't stress the concepts on the test. Talk to your instructor about his/her orientation to the course. What concepts or areas does she/he consider important? What does he/she want you to learn? Ask them to review your notes and explain where you omitted things they consider important.

Perhaps the answer was in your study notes but you didn't remember it on the test.   You can be pleased that you had it in your notes - but why didn't you remember it? Were you too tense? Do you need to recite /review more?

Perhaps you knew the answer but didn't recognize it because of the way the question was phrased. That suggests you're stressing memorization too much. Try to review with someone else. Get them to make you explain your answers and discuss ways they would say it differently. This will help you understand ideas when they are stated differently.

MORE HELP

Many schools have a learning lab or learning skills center where you can get individualized help. Ask your instructor what facilities your school provides.

Time Log

Date _____

Time	Doing what?	Where?	Comments
7:00 -		-	-
7:30 -		-	-
8:00 -		-	-
8:30 -		-	-
9:00 -		-	-
10:00 -		-	-
10:30 -		-	-
11:00 -		-	-
11:30 -		-	-
12:00 -		-	-
12:30 -		-	-
1:00 -		-	-
1:30 -		-	-
2:00 -		-	-
2:30 -		-	-
3:00 -		-	-
4:00 -		-	-
4:30 -		-	-
5:00 -		-	-
5:30 -		-	-
6:00 -		-	-
6:30 -		-	-
7:00 -		-	-
7:30 -		-	-
8:00 -		-	-
8:30 -		-	-
9:00 -		-	-
9:30 -		-	-
10:00 -		-	-
10:30 -		-	-
11:00 -		-	-
11:30 -		-	-
12:00 -		-	-

1. Introduction: Historical and Scientific Considerations

OVERVIEW

The first five chapters cover basic ideas and issues in abnormal psychology. These chapters are a background for the rest of the text which covers forms of psychopathology and related topics.

The first two chapters discuss viewpoints on the nature of psychopathology. For example, should people with psychological problems be viewed as "sick," as having "adjustment problems," or as the victims of faulty socialization or learning?

The way we view these problems becomes especially important when discussing ways of classifying and studying psychopathology - in Chapters 3, 4, and 5. For example, if we view people with these problems as being "mentally ill", then we would want to diagnose what illness the person has and develop ways to study and treat the illness. If we perceive these people instead as having trouble adjusting to society or as having learned ineffective ways of getting along in the world, then we might want to categorize and study their problems somewhat differently.

CHAPTER SUMMARY

Chapter one covers three major topics. *The Mental Health Professions* briefly describes the training, skills, and orientations of the various mental health professions.

The *History of Psychopathology* shows that different historical periods have emphasized one of three views concerning the causes of psychopathology: Demonology (caused by evil spirits), Somatogenesis (bodily causes) or Psychogenesis (psychological or mental causes). These three views have led societies to study and treat disturbed individuals in different ways.

Science: A Human Enterprise points out that science is both objective (in gathering data) and subjective (reflecting the views of the people who gather the data). That is, the paradigms or theories of scientists influence the kinds of data they seek and the way they make sense out of what they find. Paradigms can also make it difficult for scientists to recognize phenomena that don't fit their paradigm. Hypnosis is discussed both as a historical topic and as an illustration of the influence of paradigms.

ESSENTIAL CONCEPTS

1. The text takes a scientific rather than a phenomenological approach to understanding abnormal behavior.

2. There are many different types of professionals involved in the field of mental health.

3. There have been differing views on the cause of abnormal behavior throughout history although contemporary ideas basically stem from the somatogenic and the psychogenic viewpoints, which emerged 2,000 years ago and in the 18th century, respectively.

4. The way societies understand abnormal behavior strongly affects the way in which abnormal behavior is treated (e.g. trephining).

5. Past methods of treating abnormal behavior have varied and, often, been inhuman. But they may not have been as bad as portrayed nor are current practices as enlightened as sometimes depicted.

6. Although the scientific enterprise strives to be objective, it includes many elements of subjectivity, such as those involved in deciding what data to collect or what questions to ask (paradigms).

KEY TERMS
(And Historically Significant People)

Clinical psychologist (p. 6)

Psychiatrist (p. 6)

Psychoanalyst (p. 6)

Psychiatric social worker (p. 7)

Counseling psychologist (p. 7)

Psychopathologist (p. 7)

Demonology (p. 7)

Somatogenesis (p. 8)

Hippocrates (p. 8)

Zeitgeist (p. 8)

Moral treatment (p. 18)

Philippe Pinel (p. 15)

Emil Kraepelin (p. 20)

Psychogenesis (p. 20)

Anton Mesmer (p. 21)

Jean Charcot (p. 21)

Josef Breuer (p. 21)

Paradigm (p. 26)

STUDY QUESTIONS

THE MENTAL HEALTH PROFESSIONS (p. 6)

1. Describe the training of clinical psychologists, psychiatrists and psychoanalysts. (p. 6-7)

HISTORY OF PSYCHOPATHOLOGY (p. 7)

2. Which was the earliest theory of deviant behavior? How did it explain abnormality and what kinds of treatment resulted from it? (p. 7)

3. What theory of deviant behavior emerged under Hippocrates? According to this theory, what was the cause of deviance? How did treatment emphases change as a result? (p. 8)

4. How was deviant behavior viewed and treated during the dark ages?
   Were the mentally ill treated as witches?   (p. 9-12)

5. How were the mentally ill treated in early asylums?   How did this
   change with the development of moral treatment?   (p. 12-18)

6. Describe the development of contemporary views of somatogenesis
   and psychogenesis.   (Include the contributions of Kraepelin, Pasteur,
   Mesmer, Charcot and Breuer.) (p. 19-22)

SCIENCE: A HUMAN ENTERPRISE (p. 22-27)

7. By pointing out that science is a human enterprise, the text emphasizes that science is both objective and subjective. In what way is it (a) objective and (b) subjective? (p. 23, 26)

8. What is a paradigm? Why are paradigms (a) necessary and (b) potentially limiting? (p. 26)

9. Describe the work of Langer and Abelson (1974) as an example of paradigms in abnormal psychology. How does their study illustrate the role of paradigms? (p. 26-27)

SELF-TEST, CHAPTER 1
(*ed items not covered in Study Questions)

MULTIPLE-CHOICE

1. An individual with doctoral training in the scientific study of behavior as well as training and experience in psychotherapy would be called a
   a. clinical psychologist.
   b. psychiatrist.
   c. psychoanalyst.
   d. psychopathologist.

2. The oldest theory of deviant behavior attributed it to
   a. witchcraft.
   b. demonic possession.
   c. bodily malfunction.
   d. mental imbalance.

3. What kinds of treatment for deviant behavior developed with Hippocrates' somatogenic hypothesis?
   a. medicinal herbs, potions, surgery
   b. prayer, incantations, blessings from priests
   c. relaxation, healthy food, abstinence
   d. bleeding, frightening patients by dunking them in water.

4. Currently it appears that, during the dark ages, most mentally ill people were
   a. the only ones considered witches.
   b. considered witches along with sane people.
   c. treated humanely.
   d. ignored by society.

5. "Moral treatment" of the mentally ill refers to
   a. exorcising the demons they were thought to be possessed by.
   b. creating a quiet, calm atmosphere for them to live in.
   c. burning them at the stake in the name of religious beliefs.
   d. separating them from the rest of society.

6. Emil Kraepelin
   a. developed a description of human anatomy which was accepted for many years but later found to be incorrect.
   b. developed the cathartic method of treating mental illness.
   c. developed a classification system for mental illness that still influences diagnosis today.
   d. discovered that hypnosis could block pain.

*7. The germ theory of disease
   a. provided an explanation for schizophrenia which is still accepted today.
   b. clarified the connection between syphilis and symptoms of mental illness.
   c. provided evidence for the psychogenic hypothesis.
   d. has hampered progress in the field of abnormal behavior.

8. What is an implication of the fact that science is a human enterprise?
   a. Scientific facts are uncertain because scientists make mistakes
   b. Scientists can only find the facts they are prepared to find
   c. Scientific progress depends on continued public and financial support
   d. Human frailties limit the potential for space exploration

9. Paradigms are necessary in order for science to
   a. evaluate theories objectively.
   b. insure that all possible data is considered.
   c. define the methods of investigation to use.
   d. remain sensitive to the human implications of their findings.

10. Which result, in Langer and Abelson's study, demonstrated the importance of paradigms?
   a. clinicians' adjustment ratings agreed with their qualitative descriptions of the interviewee.
   b. clinicians were influenced by whether the man was described as a job applicant or a patient
   c. traditional clinicians were influenced by descriptions of the man as a patient more than behavioral therapists.
   d. the experimenters described the man as intense but uncertain.

SHORT ANSWER

*1. Students of abnormal psychology need to have great _____ because human behavior is not well understood.

2. Describe the training of a psychiatrist.

3. What kinds of treatments evolved from early demonology?

4. Hippocrates argued that deviant behavior was not punishment by the gods but the result of . . .

*5. _____ was the name of the movement during the Middle Ages in which religious leaders searched out and killed those believed to be witches.

6. How were the mentally ill treated in early asylums?

7. The _____ paradigm became prominent as an attempt to understand people who had lost sensory or motor abilities.

8. Mesmer used an early form of _____ to treat people whose magnetic fluids were, he believed, out of balance.

9. Why are paradigms potentially limiting?

10. Langer & Abelson's study illustrates the role of paradigms in psychology. Describe what they did.

ANSWERS TO SELF-TEST, CHAPTER 1

MULTIPLE-CHOICE

1. A (p. 6-7)   2. B (p. 7)   3. C (p. 8)   4. C (p. 10-12)
5. B (p. 16-18)   6. C (p. 20)   7. B (p. 20)   8. B (p. 26)
9. C (p. 26)   10. C (p. 26-27)

SHORT ANSWER

1. Tolerance for ambiguity (p. 5)

2. Trained in medicine (an M.D.) plus post-graduate supervised experience worked with disturbed individuals. (p. 6)

3. Attempts to induce the demons to leave through prayer, drive them out through torture etc. Also living a religious, healthy life. (p. 7)

4. Natural causes (p. 8)

5. The Inquisition (p. 9-10)

6. Confined with lepers and social outcasts under poor conditions. Some asylums sold tickets to people who found their behavior amusing. (p. 12-14)

7. Psychogenic (p. 20-21)

8. Hypnotism (p. 21)

9. They influence how research is done and interpreted so that biases distortions may develop. (p. 26)

10. Behavioral and psychoanalytic therapists viewed a videotape of a man described as either a job applicant or a patient. Then they rated the man's mental health. (p. 26)

2. Current Paradigms in Psychopathology and Therapy

OVERVIEW

This is the second of five introductory chapters over topics that are basic to the rest of the text. Chapter 1 discussed the role of paradigms in science and traced the paradigms that have been important in the history of psychopathology. Many of the differences underlying those paradigms are still unresolved. In particular, the relative importance of physical and psychological factors in pathology is still widely debated. As the field has developed, other distinctions have also emerged. These distinctions underlie the current paradigms in psychopathology which are described in Chapter 2. These current paradigms will be used to help understand and study the various types of psychopathology described later. Thus the paradigms reappear many times throughout the rest of the text.

Chapters 3 and 4 will deal with the topics of classification and assessment. They describe the currently used categories of psychopathology and the methods used to assess individuals who may have psychological problems. There are a number of issues and controversies involved in both classifying pathology and assessing individuals. Not surprisingly these reflect differences between the various paradigms presented in Chapters 1 and 2.

Chapter 5 will discuss research methods in psychopathology. Then the text will begin covering the major forms of abnormality.

CHAPTER SUMMARY

Chapter 2 describes five current paradigms: the physiological, psychoanalytic, learning, cognitive, and humanistic paradigms. Each paradigm is a viewpoint on how we should understand, study, and treat psychopathology. As you study the chapter, remember that these are contemporary orientations. Thus you are likely to find your own ideas about psychopathology somewhere among them.

The Physiological Paradigm is similar to the so-called "medical model". This paradigm assumes that psychopathology, like medical disease, results from an organic problem. Thus we should try to identify and correct the defect - or at least control it's symptoms.

The Psychoanalytic Paradigm originated with Sigmund Freud who looked for psychological origins of psychopathology in repressed or unconscious processes originating in childhood conflicts. Post-Freudian ego-analysts are more concerned with conscious ego processes but continue Freud's emphasis on using verbal techniques to lift repression and re-examine conflicts.

Learning Paradigms, especially behaviorism, view psychopathology as ineffective behavior acquired through principles of classical conditioning, operant conditioning, and mediational processes. Thus the emphasis is on carefully defining terms and studying behavior in detail so that the the same conditioning principles can be used to help people acquire more satisfying behaviors.

The Cognitive Paradigm considers a more complex view of learning emphasizing how individuals organize stimuli into internal schema or organized networks of knowledge. Psychopathology is viewed in terms of ineffective understandings or irrational beliefs that may be relearned. Cognitive therapists share many beliefs and techniques with behavioral therapists.

The Humanistic Paradigm argues that people are inherently worthwhile and that psychopathology develops when people become afraid to accept their inner nature. Humanistic therapists encourage clients to rediscover and trust themselves and their impulses.

The Consequences of Adopting a Paradigm are to both focus and limit the search for answers. Fortunately there are many current paradigms in abnormal psychology since our understanding is very limited. A diathesis-stress paradigm may help integrate various viewpoints by focusing on underlying physical and psychological predispositions (diatheses) to react abnormally to particular environmental stressors.

ESSENTIAL CONCEPTS

1. Currently five major paradigms (sets of assumptions) are popular ways of understanding psychopathology.

2. The physiological paradigm assumes that the roots of psychopathology are somatic in nature. This paradigm is distinguished from the so called medical model.

3. The psychoanalytic paradigm assumes psychopathology results from unconscious conflicts. It is based on Freud's ideas about the structure of the mind, the psychosexual stages of development, anxiety, and defenses.

4. The learning paradigm asserts that abnormal behavior is learned much as normal behavior is learned. It defines three major learning process: Classical and Operant conditioning, and Modeling.

5. The cognitive paradigm emphasizes unobservable processes and views the individual as an active participant in the learning process. The learning and cognitive paradigms often overlap in practice.

6. The humanistic paradigm, developed in reaction to the dominance of the psychoanalytic and learning views, asserts the innate goodness of humans and their ability to choose (and be responsible for) more satisfying styles of being.

7. Each paradigm has evolved characteristic therapeutic approaches.

8. The diathesis-stress paradigm is an attempt to integrate these paradigms in accounting for abnormal behavior.

KEY TERMS

Physiological paradigm (p. 30)

Medical model (p. 30)

Psychoanalytic paradigm (p. 32)

Id (p. 32)

Ego (p. 32-33)

Superego (p. 33)

Oral stage (p. 33)

Anal stage (p. 33)

Phallic stage (p. 33)

Latency period (p. 33)

Genital stage (p. 33)

Fixation (p. 33)

Neurotic anxiety (p. 36)

Defense mechanisms (p. 36)

Free association (p. 42)

Dream analysis (p. 42)

Analysis of defenses (p. 42)

Classical conditioning (p. 43-45)

UCS (p. 44)

UCR (p. 44)

CS (p. 44

CR (p. 44)

Extinction (p. 44)

Reinforcement (p. 45)

Operant conditioning (p. 45)

Shaping (p. 45)

Modeling (p. 46)

Mediational learning (p. 46)

Avoidance conditioning (p. 47)

Systematic desensitization (p. 48)

Token economy (p. 49)

Cognition (p. 49)

Schema (p. 49-50)

Cognitive restructuring (p. 50-51)

Rational-emotive therapy (p. 51)

Humanistic paradigm (p. 52)

Client-centered therapy (p. 53)

Unconditional positive regard (p. 54)

Empathy (p. 54)

Diathesis-stress (p. 55)

STUDY QUESTIONS

THE PHYSIOLOGICAL PARADIGM (p. 30-32)

1. How is the " physiological paradigm" both A) similar to and B) different from the "medical model"?   Are physiological treatments based on knowledge that a problem is physiologically caused? Explain. (p. 30-32)

THE PSYCHOANALYTIC PARADIGM (p. 32-42)

2. Briefly describe Freud's three mental functions and his four (or five) stages of psychosexual development.   (p. 32-33)

3. How does neurotic anxiety develop according to Freud's earlier and later theories?   (Pay attention to what is repressed in each theory.) What role do defense mechanisms play in this process?   (p. 36-37)

4. Why has classical psychoanalysis focused on lifting repression? Describe three methods for doing this.   How has the focus changed over the years?   (p. 41-42)

LEARNING PARADIGMS (p. 42-49)

5. What methods did early behaviorism oppose?   What alternative did it offer?   (p. 42-43)

6. Describe two basic conditioning paradigms.   Give examples of each. (p. 43-45)

7. How do mediational learning paradigms differ from from classical and operant paradigms?   Describe modeling (p. 46) and avoidance conditioning as examples of mediational paradigms. (p. 46-47)

8. What are two assumptions of all learning points of view regarding deviant behavior? How effective have learning views been in (1) studying abnormality and (2) identifying causes of abnormality? (p. 47-48)

9. Describe a behavior therapy procedure which is based on each of the three learning paradigms. (p. 48-4

THE COGNITIVE PARADIGM (p. 49-52)

10. How does the cognitive paradigm view the learning process? How is this fundamentally different from learning paradigms? (p. 49-50)

11. As an example of cognitive behavior therapy, briefly summarize Ellis' rational-emotive approach. Identify two ways learning and cognitive paradigms are combined by therapists. (p. 50-52)

THE HUMANISTIC PARADIGM (p. 52-54)

12. Distinguish between the humanistic and existential traditions of the humanistic paradigm. Summarize the humanistic view of human behavior in four points. (Hint: look for human nature, reason for problems, phenomenological world, and free will.) (p. 52-53)

13. What is the goal of humanistic therapies such as client-centered therapy? Describe two aspects of this approach. (p. 53-54)

CONSEQUENCES OF ADOPTING A PARADIGM (p. 55-58)

14. What does the text see as consequences of adopting a paradigm? Explain the diathesis-stress paradigm and how it may be extended to make current paradigms more flexible.   (p. 55-57)

SELF-TEST, CHAPTER 2
(*ed items not covered in the Study Questions)

MULTIPLE-CHOICE

1. Medical model is another term for the _____ paradigm.
   a. psychoanalytic
   b. humanistic
   c. physiological
   d. psychiatric

2. If an analogy were to be made between Freud's description of the structure of the mind and driving a car, the _____ would be the engine, the _____ would be the speed limit, and the _____ would be the driver.
   a. id, ego, superego
   b. id, superego, ego
   c. ego, superego, id
   d. ego, id, superego

3. According to Freud, neurotic anxiety refers to
   a. fear of danger in the external world.
   b. fear of self-punishment for breaking the moral code.
   c. fear of expressing unconscious impulses.
   d. fear of the opposite sex parent.

4. At the beginning of her first session of psychoanalytic therapy, Jane was told by her therapist to say whatever thoughts came into her mind, without censoring them. This is an example of
   a. analysis of defenses.
   b. free association.
   c. catharsis.
   d. ego analysis.

5. Bart was bitten by a dog when he was a little boy. Now whenever he sees a dog, he gets frightened. From a classical conditioning view, his fear of dogs is a(n)
   a. conditioned stimulus.
   b. unconditioned stimulus.
   c. conditioned response.
   d. unconditioned response.

6. What paradigm assumes that abnormality and normality develop in the same way?
    a. Physiological
    b. Psychoanalytic
    c. Behavioral
    d. Humanistic

7. Token economies operate on the principles of
    a. classical conditioning.
    b. operant conditioning.
    c. modeling.
    d. role playing.

8. The primary goal of cognitive behavior therapy is to
    a. modify irrational behavior.
    b. restructure maladaptive emotions.
    c. increase assertiveness.
    d. change thinking processes.

9. Which of the following is an assumption of the humanistic paradigm?
    a. People are basically good.
    b. Real maturity depends on good childhood experiences.
    c. Normal and deviant behaviors develop through the same processes.
    d. people need objective feedback on their strengths and weaknesses.

*10. The authors of the text conclude that paradigms
    a. should be diverse to encourage different perspectives.
    b. have blocked the progress of understanding abnormal behavior.
    c. are all basically the same when closely examined.
    d. are no longer necessary for progress in the field.

SHORT ANSWER

1. Why does the text prefer the term "physiological paradigm" to "medical model"?

2. What is the focus of the "anal stage"?

3. According to Freud's later theory, why are conflicts repressed?

4. How has the focus of psychoanalysis changed over the years?

5. Which operant conditioning principle is illustrated by the following? When infant Johnny said "mmm" his mother was sure he meant "mother" and hugged him..   After awhile she began hugging him only when he said "ma" and, then, only when he said "ma ma".

6. In the behavioral technique of _____ individuals are taught to relax deeply.   Then, while relaxed, they imagine situations which are increasingly anxiety provoking.

7. Cognitive psychologists are interested in studying what issues or questions?

8. In client-centered therapy what is "unconditional positive regard"?

9. The following is an example of the _____ paradigm.   College students become anxious if both (a) their parents push them very hard to make good grades and if (b) they then take very difficult courses.

10. Define "Diathesis"

ANSWERS TO SELF-TEST, CHAPTER 2

MULTIPLE-CHOICE

1. C (p. 30)   2. B (p. 32-33) 3. C (p. 36)   4. B (p. 42)
5. C (p. 43-44)   6. C (p. 47)   7. B (p. 49)   8. D (p. 50-51)
9. A (p. 52)   10. A (p. 55)

SHORT ANSWER

1. Because "medical model" is vague. Arguments often reduce to whether behavior is due to physiological processes. (p. 30)

2. Toilet training. Concerns about elimination & retention (especially of feces) (p. 33)

3. Because they generate so much anxiety. (p. 36)

4. Less emphasis on unconscious sexual id forces driving the individual and more emphasis on conscious ego decisions. (p. 38-39)

5. Shaping (p. 45)

6. Systematic desensitization (p. 48-49)

7. How people actively interpret experiences or make sense out of situations. (p. 49)

8. Making clear to clients that the therapist values and respects them as individuals irregardless of their feelings and actions.(p. 54)

9. Diathesis-stress. (p. 55-56)

10. A predisposition (physiological or psychological) to develop a problem. (p. 55)

3. Classification and Diagnosis

OVERVIEW

This is the third of five introductory chapters. The first two chapters covered historical and contemporary paradigms or theories of abnormality. The remaining three deal with less theoretical issues. Chapter 3 summarizes the standard diagnostic system for classifying disturbed individuals. It also discusses some basic issues regarding classification. Chapter 4 deals with issues and methods of assessment. Mental health professionals use these methods for both individual assessment and research. Chapter 5 will cover research methods. Chapter 5 will complete the introductory chapters.

Chapters 3, 4, and 5 are less overtly theoretical than the earlier chapters. Still, the paradigm differences continue and are reflected in differences about how best to classify and study abnormality.

CHAPTER SUMMARY

Chapter 3 discusses the standard system for categorizing psychopathology and issues concerning this system and classification in general.

DSM-IIIR - The Diagnostic System of the American Psychiatric Association summarizes the history and some general characteristics of this standard diagnostic system especially it's approach to diagnosing individuals on multiple axes or dimensions. The chapter summarizes the main categories in DSM-IIIR. Later chapters will cover these categories in detail.

Issues in the Classification of Abnormal Behavior are whether people should be classified at all and whether DSM-IIIR is a good classification system. In classifying we lose information and may stigmatize people. However some classification system is needed in order to study and treat problems. Earlier DSM systems were criticized for lack of reliability (consistency in applying labels) and validity (accuracy of the labels). DSM-IIIR appears more reliable but it's broader utility is not yet clear.

ESSENTIAL CONCEPTS

1. DSM-IIIR is quite different from earlier classification systems. It's multiaxial structure is perhaps its most distinctive innovation.

2. The range of mental disorders listed in DSM-IIIR are of such great importance that they form the basis for organizing much of the text.

3. Some critics object to the very concept of classifying abnormal behavior for several reasons.

4. Other critics see value in classifying abnormal behavior, but question the approach as well as the reliability and validity the DSM system.

5. Diagnostic reliability refers to whether or not different diagnosticians will agree on a given diagnosis.

6. Validity of a classification is measured (in three ways) by whether or not accurate statements and predictions can be made from knowledge of class materials.

7. Validity is dependent upon reliability because the more unreliable a diagnosis is, the more difficult it is to establish its validity.

8. Although DSM-IIIR is more reliable than its predecessors because it contains specific diagnostic criteria, it is still far from perfect.

KEY TERMS

DSM-IIIR (p. 62)

Multiaxial classification (p. 62)

Disorders usually first evident in infancy, childhood, or adolescence (p. 65)

Organic mental disorders (p. 65)

Psychoactive substance use disorders (p. 65)

Schizophrenia (p. 66)

Delusional paranoid disorders (p. 66)

Mood disorders (p. 66)

Anxiety disorders (p. 67)

Somatoform disorders (p. 67)

Dissociative disorders (p. 67)

Sexual disorders (p. 67)

Psychological factors affecting physical conditions (p. 67)

Sleep disorders (p. 67)

Personality disorders (p. 67)

Developmental disorders (p. 68)

Code V (p. 68)

Reliability (p. 70)

STUDY QUESTIONS

1. What do the initials "DSM-IIIR" stand for? Who publishes DSM-IIIR?
(p.62)

DSM-IIIR - THE DIAGNOSTIC SYSTEM OF THE AMERICAN PSYCHIATRIC
ASSOCIATION (p. 62-68)

2. What is DSM-IIIR's "multiaxial system"? What are the five axes and
the rationale for distinguishing them (especially axes I and II)? (p.
62-64)

3. Identify and define the major diagnostic categories involved in axes I and II (15 in all). (You may wish to refer to the glossary in the back of the text.) (p. 65-68)

ISSUES IN THE CLASSIFICATION OF ABNORMAL BEHAVIOR (p. 69-73)

4. What two general issues in the classification of abnormal behavior does the text identify? (p. 68-69)

5. Summarize two issues regarding classification per. se. by giving arguments for and against each. What general defense of classification is offered? (p. 69)

6. Briefly identify three criticisms of actual diagnostic practice. Summarize the first by giving arguments for and against. (p. 70)

7. Define "reliability". Summarize Beck et al's (1962) study on the reliability of the DSM approach. (p. 70)

8. Define "validity" and explain it's relation to "reliability". What three kinds of validity may be sought for a diagnosis? (p. 70-71)

9. How did DSM-III and DSM-IIIR attempt to respond to the criticisms above? In what area did they succeed? What five problems (may) remain? (p. 71-73)

SELF-TEST, CHAPTER 3

MULTIPLE-CHOICE

1. The classification of abnormal behavior is included in
   a. Only Axes I & II of DSM-IIIR.
   b. Only Axis I of DSM-IIIR.
   c. Only Axes III & IV of DSM-IIIR.
   d. All the DSM-IIIR Axes.

2. The Global Assessment of Functioning (GAF) Scale is used for which DSM-IIIR Axis?
   a. Axis I
   b. Axis II
   c. Axis III
   d. Axis IV
   e. Axis V

3. In DSM-IIIR _____ disorders involve inflexible and maladaptive behavior patterns such as anti-social behavior.
   a. somatoform
   b. mood
   c. dissociative
   d. personality

4. According to the text, what argument has been raised by those who oppose any attempt at classification?
   a. labeling ignores the unique qualities of each individual
   b. labeling is unfair in a democratic society
   c. classification procedures are unreliable and inaccurate
   d. labeling leads us to see pathology everywhere

5. Imagine a classification system for psychopathology in which John and Sheila are labeled as redheads, and Jake and Tom are diagnosed as excessively short. The most important problem with this system is that
   a. information about people is lost.
   b. this classification may stigmatize people.
   c. the classification system is unreliable.
   d. the dimensions being classified are irrelevant.

6. Claire was diagnosed as having schizophrenia. When she went to get a second opinion, she was told she had manic-depression. This demonstrates the problem of
   a. labeling.
   b. unreliability.
   c. lack of validity.
   d. observer bias.

7. If a classification system is unreliable,
   a. its validity will not be affected.
   b. its validity is likely to be lower.
   c. its concurrent validity will be affected, but not its predictive validity.
   d. its predictive validity will be affected, but not its concurrent validity.

8. When it was discovered that general paresis was caused by syphilis, this was a demonstration of the _____ of the classification.
   a. reliability
   b. etiological validity
   c. concurrent validity
   d. predictive validity

9. The rules for making diagnostic decisions in DSM-IIIR
   a. were determined on the basis of extensive research.
   b. were based on the view of abnormal behavior as a continuum, not as discrete entities.
   c. are more specific, but not necessarily more valid.
   d. all of the above.

10. The text criticizes DSM-IIIR for
    a. making too many behaviors into disorders.
    b. making artificial distinctions between essential and associated features.
    c. not paying attention to problems of reliability.
    d. making rules for arriving at diagnoses needlessly complex.

SHORT ANSWER

1. In DSM-IIIR, axis II is used to designate _____.

2. In DSM-IIIR _____ are characterized physical symptoms that have a psychological, not a physical, cause.

3. Define and give an example of "mood disorders".

4. The two major groups of issues in the classification of abnormal behavior are _____ and _____.

5. One possible criticism of current diagnostic practice is that it is difficult to indicate degrees of abnormality because . . .

6. A diagnostic label is _____ if diagnosticians agree on applying it to particular individuals.

7. What was the most common reason for disagreements between diagnosticians in the study by Beck and others?

8. The _____ of a diagnostic label is always limited by its _____.

9. A diagnostic label is said to have etiological validity if . . .

ANSWERS TO SELF-TEST, CHAPTER 3

MULTIPLE-CHOICE

1. A (p. 60)   2. E (p. 65)   3. D (p. 66-68)   4. A (p. 69)
5. D (p. 69)   6. B (p. 70)   7. B (p. 70)   8. B (p. 70-71)
9. C (p. 71-72)   10. A (p. 72-73)

SHORT ANSWER

1. Long term problems such as personality disorders and specific developmental disorders. (p. 62)

2. Somatoform disorders. (p. 67)

3. Disturbances of mood such as depression or mania. (p. 66)

4. The relevance of classification per se. (and) Criticisms of actual diagnostic practices. (p. 68-69, 70)

5. The labels are discrete entities (that is, people either are or are not labeled.) (p. 70)

6. Reliable (p. 70)

7. Inadequacies in the diagnostic system. (p. 70)

8. Validity.   Reliability. (p. 70)

9. The same historical causes are found in individuals given the label. (p. 70-71)

4. Clinical Assessment Procedures

OVERVIEW

This is the fourth of five introductory chapters over basic issues in psychopathology. The first two chapters covered historical and contemporary paradigms or theories of abnormality. Chapter 3 dealt with DSM-IIIR, the standard system for classifying abnormality, and then went on to summarize general issues regarding classification.

This chapter will cover the major methods used to assess and classify behavior as well as issues underlying these methods. The issues involve both paradigm differences (discussed in Chapters 1 and 2) and issues of reliability and validity (discussed in Chapter 3).

Chapter 5 will cover research methods and will complete the introductory chapters. Research issues have been included in earlier chapters (and will appear throughout the text). Chapter 5 brings these issues together by showing the relative strengths and limitations of various research approaches.

CHAPTER SUMMARY

Chapter 4 describes methods of assessing individuals and their problems in order to develop appropriate treatment programs. The first three sections describe basic assessment procedures.

Assessment of Psychopathology covers the traditional assessment methods: clinical interviews, and personality tests including projective tests, personality inventories, and intelligence tests. The chapter describes each method and then discusses problems in using it. The problems concern both the paradigms underlying these methods and problems with the reliability and validity of the methods. (Intelligence tests are covered in more detail in Chapter 16)

Assessment of Brain Abnormalities describes both medical and neuropsychological methods of assessing brain damage. Again both the methods and limitations of these procedures are described.

Behavioral Assessment procedures gather information using an SORC model. Four behavioral methods are described: direct observation, interviews & self-reports, cognitive assessment and physiological measures. Based on the behavioral paradigm, these procedures look for specific individual responses to particular situations rather than global or underlying traits as do the traditional methods above. Behaviorists hope that studying specific problem behaviors will lead them more directly to procedures for changing the behaviors. Reliability and validity issues in behavioral assessment are discussed.

Behavioral assessment methods bring up the issue of whether people's actions are the result of underlying traits or the particular situation. *The Consistency and Variability of Behavior* focuses directly on this issue.

ESSENTIAL CONCEPTS

1. The clinical interview is a widely used assessment method for observing an individual and establishing rapport. Most interview are largely unstructured and results depend on a variety of factors.

2. Projective tests rely on individuals projecting their personality as they respond to ambiguous stimuli. The unstructured nature of these tests raises questions concerning validity and reliability.

3. Personality inventories are more structured self-report measures but are limited by various problems of all self-report data.

4. Neuropsychological tests can reveal information about subtle brain damage by relying on knowledge of how brain structures effect behavior.

5. Behavioral assessment procedures emphasize situational determinates of behavior (while traditional procedures emphasize traits as determinates).

6. Although direct observation is the hallmark of the behavioral approach, self-report, cognitive, and physiological measures also are used.

7. In addition to an emphasis on situations, behavioral assessment is more treatment focused and more direct than other forms of assessment - though reliability and validity problems remain.

8. Professionals continue to debate the degree to which behavior is determined by situations or by traits.

KEY TERMS

Assessment procedures (p. 76)

Clinical interview (p. 76)

Rapport (p. 76)

Standardization (p. 80)

Projective technique (p. 80)

Projective hypothesis (p. 80)

Personality inventories (p. 81)

Intelligence test (p. 84)

Neuropsychological test (p. 86)

Situational determinants (vs. traits) (p. 88)

SORC (p. 89)

Reactivity (p. 92)

Psychophysiology (p. 95)

External validity (p. 103)

Rosenthal effect (p. 103)

STUDY QUESTIONS

ASSESSMENT OF PSYCHOPATHOLOGY (p. 76-85)

1. Describe five factors which influence the results of a clinical interview.   (p. 76-78)

2. What is the basic idea (the projective hypothesis) behind projective personality tests?   Briefly discuss their effectiveness.   (p. 80-81)

3. How are personality inventories (especially the MMPI) developed and refined into "scales" (three steps)? What are two kinds of problems with inventories and how are they handled? (p. 81-84)

4. What are/were intelligence tests designed to measure? (Is this your understanding of the term "intelligence"?) What two points does the text stress in evaluating these tests? (p. 84-85)

ASSESSMENT OF BRAIN ABNORMALITIES (p. 85-88)

5. Explain why brain dysfunctions can be hard to detect by "seeing" the brain (medically). What are neuropsychological tests and how are they used? (p. 85-88)

BEHAVIORAL ASSESSMENT (p. 88-103)

6. Explain how paradigm differences lead behaviorists to focus on situational determinants rather than traits as the causes of behavior? Describe the behavioral (SORC) approach to assessment. (p. 88-89)

7. Describe four methods of behavioral assessment. Include particular ways in which behaviorists have used each and any problems involved. (p. 89-98)

8. Explain how behavioral assessment yields a closer link between assessment and intervention. Describe two factors that influence the reliability and four factors that influence the validity of behavioral measures. (p. 98-103)

THE CONSISTENCY AND VARIABILITY OF BEHAVIOR (p. 103-107)

9. Summarize Mischel's and Wachtel's position on the determinants of behavior. What has research suggested about their positions? (p. 103-107)

SELF-TEST, CHAPTER 4

MULTIPLE-CHOICE

1. The following technique is used by most clinicians to help a client open up during a clinical interview:
   a. empathic statements
   b. catharsis
   c. the empty-chair technique
   d. free association

2. The projective hypothesis fits with the _____ paradigm.
   a. psychoanalytic
   b. learning
   c. humanistic
   d. all of the above

3. One step in the process of developing personality inventories such as the MMPI is to
   a.identify items which discriminate people with a specific type of mental disorder.
   b. select ambiguous stimuli.
   c.eliminate items which are too obvious in their content.
   d. analyze pilot data using the SORC model.

4. One problem with the self-report nature of the MMPI is the influence of
   a. situational factors like the sex of the examiner.
   b. the examinee's level of intelligence.
   c. social desirability.
   d. unstructured stimuli on the examinee.

5. One problem with intelligence tests is that they
   a. are known to be unreliable.
   b. are known to be invalid.
   c. do a poor job of predicting school performance.
   d. do not capture all relevant aspects of our notions about what intelligence is.

6. Neuropsychological tests
   a. are generally inferior to brain-scanning methods.
   b. may pick up brain damage not detectable by a neurological exam.
   c. are incompatible with neurological testing methods.
   d. are more reliable but less valid than neurological tests.

7. Tommy is usually with his mother, not his father, when he has a tantrum. In the acronym SORC, Tommy's mother is an example of the
   a. S
   b. O
   c. R
   d. C

8. What problem in behavioral assessment is illustrated by the following? Observing school phobic children, Dr X's data supports his hypothesis that parents reinforce the behavior while Dr Y's data supports her hypothesis that abusive teachers are the cause.
   a. reactivity
   b. content analysis
   c. ecological validity
   d. the Rosenthal effect

9. When directly observing behavior what is "reactivity"?
   a. a change in behavior because it is being observed
   b. the reaction of the individual observed
   c. the sensitivity of the measure used
   d. a potential for uncontrollable behavior

10. "The consistency and variability of behavior" is an argument over the relative importance of _____ and _____ in abnormality.
   a. research and clinical insight
   b. traits and environment
   c. physiology and psychology
   d. reliability and validity

SHORT ANSWER

1. Give an example of the way in which situational factors may alter results of a clinical interview.

2. Why has it been difficult to evaluate the effectiveness of projective tests?

3. What type of items are used in lie scales of personality inventories such as the MMPI?

4. Intelligence tests are designed to measure or predict . . .

5. What is the rationale for selecting the behaviors measured by neuropsychological tests?

6. Traditional assessment concentrates on _____ while behavioral assessment concentrates on situational determinates of behavior.

7. In the method of "direct observation of behavior" behavioral therapists not only watch the behavior but also . . .

8. Behavioral therapists may use physiological measures in order to get a more complete picture of . . . .

9. The _____ of behavioral assessment has been shown to depend on the complexity of the task and the conscientiousness of the observers.

10. The _____ of a behavioral assessment refers to whether the assessment applies to the real-world situations of interest.

ANSWERS TO SELF-TEST, CHAPTER 4

MULTIPLE-CHOICE

1. A (p. 76)   2. A (p. 80)   3. A (p. 82)   4. C (p. 83)
5. D (p. 84-85)   6. B (p. 86)   7. A (p. 89)   8. D (p. 103)
9. A (p. 92)   10. B (p. 103-105)

SHORT ANSWER

1. Any example in which the client's responses are influenced by factors such as the clinicians age, sex, manner, the circumstances surrounding the interview, etc. (p. 76)

2. Projective tests allow complex, open-ended responses that are difficult to categorize and analyze. (p. 80)

3. Items that people might like to endorse but cannot do so honestly (p. 83)

4. Who will succeed in school. (p. 84)

5. Select behaviors known to be related to particular brain structures. (p. 86)

6. Personality structures or traits (p. 88)

7. Analyze the sequences using behavioral terms or concepts. (p. 89)

8. emotional responses to situations (p. 95-96)

9. Reliability (p. 99)

10. External or ecological validity (p. 103)

5. Research Methods in the Study of Abnormal Behavior

OVERVIEW

Earlier chapters have covered paradigms or theories in psychopathology (Chapters 1 & 2) and classification and assessment issues (Chapters 3 & 4). Chapter 5 discusses scientific methods and research designs in abnormal psychology.

Many research issues have already been mentioned in Chapters 1 thru 4. In fact, it may have seemed that scientific research creates more confusion than answers. Research can be complex, at least in part because scientists are very concerned about the limitations of their approach and their methods. It is said that there is no perfect research design. Each has both strengths and limitations. Chapter 5 provides a background for understanding the research evidence regarding various problem behaviors in the rest of the text.

Chapter 5 is the last introductory chapter. Chapter 6 begins the first of several parts of the text which discuss various specific forms of abnormality.

CHAPTER SUMMARY

Chapter 5 discusses the methods scientists use to develop systematic knowledge as a basis for developing and evaluating theories and principles.

Science and Scientific Methods discusses basic principles of science. Statements and ideas must be publicly testable and able to be proven false. Observations must be reliable or repeatable. Theories are propositions which both result from research and generate testable ideas for further research.

The Research Methods of Abnormal Psychology include epidemiological research, case studies, correlational studies, and three forms of experiments. These methods vary in the kinds of data they produce and the ease with which inferences, especially about causes, can be drawn.

Epidemiological research studies how an illness is distributed across the population. Such studies can be helpful in planning treatment needs as well as suggesting possible causes for a problem.

The case study is an extensive description of a particular, often unusual, problem or procedure. Case studies document unusual events and suggest hypotheses for further research. It is difficult to develop general principles from them but they can provide examples to disconfirm principles.

Correlational methods measure the relationship between two (or more) variables (for example between course grades and anxiety). They are widely used in abnormal psychology but, because they do not change variables, it is difficult draw conclusions about causation from them.

In experiments one (or more) independent variables are actually changed and the effects of the change on dependent variable(s) are studied. Experiments are preferred for studying causation. However, in abnormal psychology, many variables cannot be manipulated for practical or ethical reasons. Features of experimental designs are described. Variables may be manipulated using control groups, single-subjects, or mixed designs.

ESSENTIAL CONCEPTS

1. Science is the pursuit of systematized knowledge through observation, although it is not purely objective and is influenced by time and convention.

2. In order to be considered scientific, theories must be testable or falsifiable and reliable.

3. Epidemiological research investigates the frequency and distribution of some problem in the population. Such research is useful for social planning and can suggest causes of a problem.

4. The case study lacks control and objectivity, but it can be useful for 1) describing unusual phenomena, 2) disconfirming supposedly universal aspects of a theory and, 3) generating hypothesis.

5. The correlational method is a valuable method for systematically studying the association between two or more variables but causal inferences are risky because of possible third variables and reverse causality interpretations.

6. Statistical significance refers to a convention adopted by scientists wherein a finding is not considered to be reliable unless the odds are less than 5 in 100 that it occurred by chance. Statistical significance does not guarantee social significance.

7. The experiment, when properly conducted, is a powerful tool for determining causality, although ethical and practical problems often prohibit it's use in studying psychopathology.

8. The basic features of the experiment include the experimental hypothesis, independent variables, dependent variables, experimental effects, control groups, and random assignment.

9. Internal validity refers to whether the results obtained can be confidently attributed to the independent variable. External validity concerns whether the results of a particular study are generalizable.

10. Analogue experiments are frequently used to study psychopathology but their external validity is always of concern.

11. A diagnosis is a classificatory variable so all comparisons made between diagnostic groups are correlation studies.

KEY TERMS

Theory (p. 110)

Epidemiology (p. 113)

Case study (p. 113-114)

Idiographic (p. 116)

Nomothetic (p. 116)

Correlational method (p. 116)

Correlation coefficient (r) (p. 117)

Statistical significance (p. 117)

Classificatory variable (p. 118)

Directionality problem (p. 119)

Third variable problem (p. 119-120)

High-risk method (p. 119)

The experiment (p. 120)

Experimental hypothesis (p. 120)

Independent variable (p. 120-121)

Dependent variable (p. 121)

Experimental effect (p. 121)

Internal validity (p. 121)

Control group (p. 121)

Confounds (p. 121)

Random assignment (p. 122)

Double-blind (p. 122)

External validity (p. 122)

Analogue experiment (p. 123)

Single-subject design (p. 124)

Reversal (ABAB) design (p. 124)

Multiple-baseline design (p. 124)

Mixed design (p. 126)

STUDY QUESTIONS

SCIENCE AND SCIENTIFIC METHODS (p. 110-112)

1. Describe three contemporary criteria for evaluating scientific observations and theories. Identify two advantages of (good) theories. (p. 110-112)

THE RESEARCH METHODS OF ABNORMAL PSYCHOLOGY (p. 112-127)

2.   What is epidemiology?   Describe two uses of epidemiological research. (p. 113)

3. What is done in a case study?   Describe three ways in which case studies are useful.   (p. 113-116)

4. What kind of questions do correlational methods ask?   How are the results expressed and their importance evaluated? (p. 116-118)

5. How are correlational methods often applied to psychopathology? Describe two problems with these methods. (p. 118-120)

6. Identify four basic features of the experimental design. How is this method different from the correlational method? How is this helpful in determining causality? (p. 120-121)

7. Describe how "control groups", "random assignment", and "double-blinds" are used to eliminate "confounds" and secure "internal validity" (p. 121-122)

8. What is "external validity" and why is it difficult to demonstrate? (p. 122-123)

9. What is an analogue experiment? What is the advantage and the disadvantage of using analogues in experimental designs? (p. 123-124)

10. Describe two major types of single-subject experimental designs? In what way is it difficult to generalize the results of single-subject research? (p. 124-125)

11. What is a mixed design? Identify an advantage and a disadvantage
    of mixed designs (p. 126-127)

SELF-TEST, CHAPTER 5

MULTIPLE-CHOICE

1. What two criteria for evaluating scientific theories and data are
   emphasized in the text?
   a. reliability and objectivity
   b. realism and external validity
   c. testability and reliability
   d. internal validity and explanatory power

2. Epidemiological research is helpful for
   a. understanding the phenomenology of disorders.
   b. determining the effectiveness of different treatments.
   c. planning for health-care needs of communities.
   d. idiographic analysis of diseases.

3. Case studies are of little value in
   a. comparing the effectiveness of treatments
   b. suggesting possibilities for further research
   c. proving exceptions to theories
   d. describing unusual phenomena

4. Dr. Blair compared the performance of men and women on a
   laboratory test of spatial ability. This is an example of a(n)
   a. case study.
   b. correlational study.
   c. experiment.
   d. mixed design.

5. Professor X collects data showing a correlation between grades and
   happiness. He concludes that being happy helps students to get better
   grades. Which of the following illustrates the "directionality
   problem" in Professor X's conclusion?
   a. Students with poor grades may drop out of school.
   b. Students in love may be happier and get better grades.
   c. Female (or male) students may get better grades.
   d. Good grades may produce happiness.

6. In a study about the effectiveness of two medications, if the
   subjects and the person prescribing the medication do not know who
   receives which medication, the study is
   a. externally valid.
   b. confounded.
   c. double-blind.
   d. analogue.

7. External validity is dealt with through
   a. random assignment to control groups.
   b. double-blind procedures.
   c. analogue experiments.
   d. repetition in different circumstances.

8. Probably the major question raised about analogue experiments is
   their
   a. reliability.
   b. confounded variables.
   c. internal validity.
   d. external validity.

9. In single-subject research a _____ design involves repeatedly
   applying and removing the same treatment.
   a. multiple-baseline
   b. reversal
   c. mixed
   d. correlational

10. A researcher compares the responses of schizophrenics and manic-
    depressives to a new medication vs. a placebo. This is an example of
    a(n)
    a. epidemiological design.
    b. analogue experiment.
    c. correlational study.
    d. mixed design.

SHORT ANSWER

1. What is the advantage of a (good) theory over simply describing
   observed data?

2. A study of the relationship between years of driving experience and frequency of auto accidents would be likely to find a correlation coefficient between (what two numbers?) . . .

3. Why are correlational methods commonly used in studying psychopathology?

4. What characteristic of experimental designs makes them different from correlational designs?

5. Experiments are said to be internally valid if . . .

6. Professor Jones finds that females get better scores than males on his essay tests. He would like to prove this happens because they give better answers - not because of sexual bias on his part. Describe a double-blind procedure he could use to do this.

7. What single-subject research design is illustrated by the following? To study the effect of diet on running, Joe records how fast he runs each day while he eats junk food or a well-balanced diet on alternating weeks.

8. Describe a multiple baseline design that you and a friend could use to see if filling out the study guide helps in taking tests?

9. Briefly describe a general limitation of all single-subject designs.

10. Give an example of a mixed research design.

ANSWERS TO SELF-TEST, CHAPTER 5

MULTIPLE-CHOICE

1. C (p. 110)   2. C (p. 113)   3. A (p. 114-116) 4. B (p. 116)
5. D (p. 119)   6. C (p. 122)   7. D (p. 122)   8. D (p. 123-124)
9. B (p. 124)   10. D (p. 126-127)

SHORT ANSWER

1. A theory can account for many relationships, bridge relations, etc. Thus we can account for a great number of observations with a few theoretical concepts.(p. 110-111)

2. Zero and -1.00 (assuming that more experienced drivers have fewer accidents. (p. 117)

3. Because many variables of interest in psychopathology are classificatory variables that cannot be manipulated for practical or ethical reasons. (p. 118-119)

4. Independent variable is actually manipulated/changed. (p. 120-121)

5. Effect can be confidently attributed to independent variable. (p. 121)

6. Professor Jones could have someone else, who will not be involved in grading the tests, remove all names and identifying information from the test papers before he scores them.   (p. 122)

7. Reversal or ABAB design (p. 124)

8. On the first & third test you fill out the study guide while your friend does so on the second & fourth test. (p. 124-125)

9. It is difficult to generalize the results.   That is, to show that the same results would be obtained from other individuals. (p. 125)

10. Your example should include two independent variables, one of which is simply measured (a classificatory variable) and one of which is manipulated. For example: compare test scores of male and female students (a classificatory variable) after they spend two hours hearing a lecture or reading the text (a manipulation). (p. 126-127)

6. Anxiety Disorders

OVERVIEW

The first five chapters have discussed a number of basic ideas and issues in abnormal psychology. These concepts provide a framework for surveying the various forms of abnormality. You will want to refer back to these chapters periodically as you study the rest of the text.

Chapters 6 through 17 survey the forms of abnormality. They are divided into four major groups which are:

Part 2: Emotional Disorders and Reactions to Stress such as phobias, memory loss, and ulcers,

Part 3: Social Problems such as anti-social individuals, alcohol and drug problems, and sexual problems,

Part 4: Schizophrenia characterized by confused thinking and being out of contact with reality,

Part 5: Developmental Disorders such as hyperactivity, mental retardation, and problems of the elderly.

Part 6, which is the last four chapters in the text, discusses methods of treatment as well as legal and ethical issues in treatment. Although treatments are mentioned in discussing each problem, these last chapters deal with treatment more systematically.

Now would be a good time to look over the topics of all these chapters. Notice that they cover a wide range of problem behaviors, from seemingly bizarre problems such as schizophrenia to relatively normal problems such as sexual dysfunctions. A number of them are matters of contemporary social debate, such as intelligence and retardation.

Chapters 6 thru 9 (Part 2 of the text) cover problems that are related to anxiety, emotions, and stress. Chapter 6 deals with anxiety disorders characterized directly by anxiety. Chapters 7 and 8 discuss disorders in which emotionality and stress lead to other problems. In Chapter 7 these problems are physical complaints of being blind, lame, in pain, etc. (Somatoform Disorders) or disruptions of memory, consciousness, and identity (Dissociative Disorders). In Chapter 8 they appear as physical tissue change and damage such as in ulcers and heart disease.   Finally Chapter 9 discusses Affective Disorders including depression, mania, and suicide.

CHAPTER SUMMARY

Chapter 6 begins the survey by discussing anxiety disorders.   In studying the chapter, look for the format described below (Notes to Students, 2).   Three kinds of anxiety disorders are discussed.

Phobias   are relatively common disorders involving intense, unreasonable, disruptive, fears of particular situations.   They include simple phobias such as fear of snakes, agoraphobia or fear of being away from one's home and familiar surroundings and social phobia or fear of public embarrassment.   Psychoanalysts view phobias as defenses against repressed conflicts.   Behaviorists have offered avoidance, modeling and operant   models for the development of phobias.   Physiologically oriented researchers suggest that autonomic nervous system lability (becoming physiologically aroused easily) constitutes a diathesis or predisposition for these problems.   Each has led to corresponding treatments.

Panic Disorders   are sudden, unexpected, attacks of anxiety.   Research is limited but suggests that these people escalate minor worries into full-blown panic due to physical or psychological factors.   People with *Generalized Anxiety Disorder*   live in relatively constant tension. People with *Obsessive-compulsive Disorders*   are bothered by unwanted thoughts (obsessions) and/or feel compelled to engage in repetitive rituals (compulsions) lest they be overcome by anxiety.   There are psychoanalytic, behavioral and physiological (and, occasionally, other) views on the cause of each   disorder which have led to corresponding treatments.

Posttraumatic Stress Disorder   reflects a recognition that traumatic events such as disasters or combat may effect anyone.   Aftereffects include anxiety, a numbing feeling of being separate from others, and intrusive vivid memories.   Although the disorder existed in earlier wars, recent interest has focused on the Vietnam War where both combat conditions and anti-war sentiment at home were stressful.   For Vietnam veterans treatment has focused on self-help "rap groups".

ESSENTIAL CONCEPTS

1. Anxiety disorders used to be called neuroses based on the psychoanalytic view that anxiety is caused by unconscious conflict

2. The major categories of anxiety disorders listed in DSM-IIIR are; phobias, panic disorder, generalized anxiety disorder, obsessive-compulsive disorder and posttraumatic stress disorder.

3. A phobia is a disrupting, fear-mediated avoidance, out of proportion to the actual danger from the particular object or situation that is feared.

4. Psychoanalytic theory focuses on the content of phobias - their symbolic meaning, while learning theory focuses on their function - the avoidance of a feared situation.

5. Panic disorders, involving unexpected attacks of anxiety, may result from the way people interpret physiological states.

6. Generalized anxiety disorder characterized by chronic anxiety has, often, been viewed and treated in ways similar to phobias.

7. Obsessive-compulsive disorder involves obsessive thoughts and compulsive behaviors.

8. Psychoanalysts have, generally, viewed these disorders as resulting from repression and/or unwanted impulses. Treatment seeks to lift the repression and, confront the fear directly.

9. Behaviorists have, in various ways, viewed these disorders as avoidance responses, as reinforced, or as resulting from cognitive distortions. They have developed corresponding treatments.

10. Physiological and genetic factors have been investigated and somatic treatments (especially tranquillizers) have been used.

11. Posttraumatic stress disorder, found in many Vietnam veterans, refers to the aftereffects of experiencing disasters.

NOTES TO STUDENTS

1. This is a good time to warn you of a common experience among students studying abnormal psychology. Often, students in these courses come to believe they have the problem covered in each chapter. For example, you may think you have an anxiety disorder when studying Chapter 6, depression in Chapter 9, and schizophrenia in Chapter 14. If this happens to you, don't be surprised. The various problems covered in the text are probably exaggerations of very normal tendencies in all of us. If you can see tendencies in yourself, it probably means you have developed a meaningful understanding of the problem. Of course, if you are seriously concerned, you can discuss the matter with your instructor or someone at your school's counseling center. They are used to such situations and you may be surprised at how easily they understand your concerns.

2. As you study these chapters you will discover that each follows the same general outline. First, the problem is defined and any issues regarding it's classification in DSM-IIIR are discussed. Second, theories and research into its causes are described. Typically this description includes the Psychoanalytic, Behavioral, and Physiological paradigms. Finally, various treatments are summarized under the same three paradigms. Of course the outline varies but you will find it helpful to look for this kind of outline as you study each chapter and to organize your studying around it.

KEY TERMS

Neuroses (p. 132)

Anxiety disorder (p. 132)

Phobia (p. 133)

Simple phobia (p. 135)

Agoraphobia (p. 135)

Social phobia (p. 136)

Vicarious conditioning (p. 138)

Vulnerability schema (p. 140)

Autonomic lability (p. 141)

Systematic desensitization (p. 144)

Flooding (p. 145)

Anxiolytics (p. 146)

Panic disorder (p. 146)

Depersonalization (p. 146)

Derealization (p. 146)

Generalized anxiety disorder (p. 147-148)

Helplessness (p. 148)

Gestalt therapy (p. 152)

Obsessive-compulsive disorder (p. 152)

Obsession (p. 152-153)

Compulsion (p. 153)

Posttraumatic stress disorder (p. 157)

STUDY QUESTIONS

1. Define "neuroses" pointing out the theoretical assumptions involved. How has DSM-IIIR dealt with this term? (p. 132)

PHOBIAS (p. 133-146)

2. What are phobias and why have psychologists disagreed on subclassifying them?   Describe three subcategories of phobias. (p. 133-136)

3. Summarize one Freudian and three behavioral theories of phobias with the criticisms of each (p. 136-140)

4. Summarize three models of social phobia developed out of research on social anxiety. (p. 140-141)

5. What physiological factor might be a diathesis for phobias (or other anxiety disorders)?   Describe and critique the genetic studies supporting this possibility. (p. 141-144)

6. Summarize the psychoanalytic and three behavioral approaches (desensitization, operant shaping & cognitive) to therapy for phobias. What do all these techniques have in common? What is the principal problem with the common somatic treatment? (p. 144-146)

PANIC DISORDER (p. 146-147)

7. Describe the characteristics of panic disorder. Describe how MVP syndrome and hyperventilation may lead to panic disorder (p. 146-147)

GENERALIZED ANXIETY DISORDER (p. 147-152)

8. Describe the characteristics of generalized anxiety disorder and six views on it's cause. (For the last, distinguish between neurobiological mechanisms of panic and generalized anxiety.) (p. 147-150)

9. Summarize five treatment approaches (including the community approach). (p. 150-152) (You will find it helpful to compare these treatments to the views on causes generalized anxiety as well as treatment of phobias.)

OBSESSIVE-COMPULSIVE DISORDER (p. 152-157)

10. Define and give several examples of obsessions and compulsions. How are these definitions different from way we commonly use the terms? (p. 152-154)

11. Briefly summarize four views on the causes of obsessive-compulsive disorders. (p. 154-156)

12. Briefly summarize four treatments for obsessive-compulsive disorders (One psychoanalytic, two behavioral, and one physiological). How effective is each? (Note that each is a result of one of the causal views above) (p. 156-157)

POSTTRAUMATIC STRESS DISORDER (p. 157-164)

13. What are the characteristics of posttraumatic stress disorder (PTSD)? Discuss the importance of environmental and personality factors in PTSD. (p. 157-158)

14. In the Vietnam War what combat and social stresses contributed to PTSD? How have professionals (especially in the Veterans Administration) and veterans themselves dealt with the problem? (p. 158-164)

SELF TEST, CHAPTER 6

MULTIPLE-CHOICE

1. Behaviorists have often ignored the _____ of phobias.
   a. importance
   b. content
   c. function
   d. consequences

2. Which model suggests that phobias develop when a neutral stimulus is paired with a traumatic event so that escaping the stimulus becomes reinforcing?
   a. Freudian
   b. cognitive
   c. operant conditioning
   d. avoidance conditioning

3. According to research findings, which of the following is likely to lead to social anxiety?
   a. physical unattractiveness
   b. public embarrassment
   c. observing others who are socially anxious
   d. poor social skills

4. Advice for phobics to confront the feared object in real life is given by
   a. ego analysts.
   b. behavior therapists.
   c. cognitive therapists.
   d. all of the above.
   e. none of the above.

5. Mitral valve prolapse (MVP) syndrome has been found to be common in patients with the following disorder:
   a. simple phobia
   b. panic disorder
   c. generalized anxiety disorder
   d. posttraumatic stress disorder

6. According to research findings, which of the following situations would probably cause the <u>most</u> anxiety, given that all resulted in the same amount of electric shock being administered?
   a. receiving shocks from the experimenter.
   b. administering shocks to yourself.
   c. receiving shocks from the experimenter which you can terminate by pushing a button.
   d. observing a confederate being shocked by the experimenter.

7. The purpose of the empty-chair technique is to
   a. highlight the conflict between the client's two self-concepts.
   b. have the client adopt his or her's parents' perspective regarding early childhood experiences.
   c. help the client move away from the present anxiety and imagine a more relaxed, calm approach to life.
   d. increase awareness by forcing an individual to confront basic wants and fears.

8. An irresistible impulse to repeat some ritualistic act over and over is called
   a. an obsession.
   b. a compulsion.
   c. an irrational belief.
   d. a schema.

9. In the psychoanalytic view, what is the cause of obsessive-compulsive disorders?
   a. struggles to control instinctual impulses
   b. excessive control of id energies
   c. reawakened childhood Oedipal fears
   d. repressed conflicts are displaced to symbolically related situations

10. What do behaviorists do to treat compulsions?
    a. prevent reinforcement of the behavior
    b. punish the behavior when it occurs
    c. stop the behavior from occurring
    d. shape new alternative behaviors

SHORT ANSWER

1. What assumption was the basis for the term "neuroses"?

2. Define "social phobia" distinguishing it from agoraphobia.

3. List three theoretical possibilities which have been considered in research on social anxiety.

4. Describe what is done in systematic desensitization as a treatment for phobias.

5. In what way are panic disorder and generalized anxiety disorder similar?

6. What is the basis for generalized anxiety according to cognitive-behavioral views?

7. Summarize humanistic views on the cause of anxiety.

8. What is done in behavioral treatment of anxiety?

9. What are the characteristics of posttraumatic stress disorder (PTSD)?

10. What topics are commonly discussed in rap sessions held to help Vietnam veterans deal with stress reactions?

ANSWERS TO SELF-TEST, CHAPTER 6

MULTIPLE-CHOICE

1. B (p. 134)   2. D (p. 136-137) 3. D (p. 140-141) 4. D (p. 144-146)
5. B (p. 146-147) 6. A (p. 149)   7. D (p. 152)   8. B (p. 153)
9. A (p. 155)   10. C (p. 155)

SHORT ANSWER

1. Freudian assumption that many problems were based, directly or indirectly, on repressed anxiety. (p. 132)

2. Unreasonable fear of public scrutiny or embarrassment. (As distinguished from agoraphobia or fear of public, unfamiliar situations.) (p. 135-136)

3. 1) Unfortunate social experiences, 2) lack of social skills, 3) irrational beliefs - such as "It's awful if someone does not approve of me." (p. 140-141)

4. Individual is taught how to relax deeply. Then, while relaxed, person experiences (perhaps, by imagining them) a series of gradually more fearful situations. (p. 144)

5. Person experiences anxiety which is not linked to a particular situation. (p. 146-148)

6. Helplessness or lack of control over events. (p. 148)

7. Anxiety develops as we accept others negative opinions rather than our own natural, positive, opinions of ourselves. (p. 149)

8. Identify & treat causes of anxiety through desensitization, teaching skills, etc. (p. 150-152)

9. Difficulty concentrating, relaxing, sleeping. Psychic numbing or loss of interest, flashbacks. (p. 157)

10. Feelings about the war (guilt, anger) about family life (social and family changes), and society's attitudes toward the war. (p. 163-164)

7. Somatoform and Dissociative Disorders

OVERVIEW

Chapter 7 is the second of four chapters on emotional disorders and reactions to stress. The previous chapter discussed disorders involving fairly direct struggles with anxiety. These included chronic anxiety, phobias or unreasonable fears, and obsessions and compulsions in which people think and do things in order to control anxiety.

Chapters 7 and 8 describe disorders in which people may not directly complain of anxiety but have other problems that appear related to anxiety and stress in some way. In Chapter 8 the other problems involve physical damage and tissue change such as an ulcer (Psychophysiological Disorders). In Chapter 7 the other problems are physical complaints such as complaints of pain or inability to walk (somatoform disorders) or are problems of memory, consciousness, and identity such as amnesia (dissociative disorders).

Chapter 9 concludes this part of the text by discussing disorders of affect involving feelings such as depression. Then a new part of the text begins which covers social problems including criminality, drug abuse, and sexual problems.

CHAPTER SUMMARY

Chapter 7 covers two groups of disorders in which there is a loss of functioning with no physical basis. The symptoms seem to serve a psychological purpose.

Somatoform Disorders are characterized by physical complaints which have no physiological basis. They include two disorders. In conversion disorders there is a loss of sensory or motor functioning. For example; a loss of vision, touch, etc. or of the ability to walk, talk, etc. In somatization disorder there are multiple physical complaints (headaches, various pains, fatigue, etc) involving repeated visits to physicians and medical treatment.

Theories of somatoform disorders deal primarily with conversions. Psychoanalysts propose that repressed conflicts are "converted" into the physical symptoms in various ways and seek to uncover the impulses.   Behavioral theorists suggest that people are reinforced for being in the role of a "sick" person and seek to reduce anxiety while teaching more socially effective behaviors.   Sociocultural, genetic, and physiological views have also been offered.

Dissociative Disorders are disorders of awareness and memory.   In psychogenic amnesia the individual is unable to recall important personal information; often of traumatic events.   Psychogenic fugue involves a more encompassing memory loss in which the person leaves home and assumes a new identity.   In multiple personality two or more separate and distinct personalities occur in alternation, each having it's own memories, behaviors, and life styles.

Psychoanalysis suggests that dissociative disorders reflect a massive repression of memory or identity that protects the individual when repressed conflicts have broken through into awareness.   Similarly, behavioral theory describes dissociative disorders as avoidance responses motivated by anxiety.   Thus both propose that treatment focus on the anxiety that presumably provoked the problem.

ESSENTIAL CONCEPTS

1. Conversion disorder and somatization disorder are two major categories of somatoform disorders.

2. In conversion disorders muscular or sensory functions are impaired but there is no apparent physical basis so that the symptoms seem to be linked to psychological factors.

3. It is difficult to distinguish conversion disorders from physical illnesses or from malingering.

4. Somatization disorder is characterized by recurrent, multiple somatic complaints for which medical attention is sought but which have no apparent physical basis.

5. Conversion disorders occupy a central place in psychoanalytic thinking because their nature leads one to consider the concept of the unconscious.

6. While Freud allowed for secondary gain or direct reinforcement for the symptoms of a conversion disorder, he suggested that the primary gain was avoidance of repressed id impulses.

7. Behaviorists suggest that conversions reflect the way the individual understands "sick" people behave.

8. The dissociative disorders include psychogenic amnesia, psychogenic fugue, and multiple personality.

9. The dissociative disorders suggest the plausibility of Freud's concept of repression.

10. Little is known about the relative efficacy of treatments for either somatoform   or dissociative disorders.

KEY TERMS

Somatoform disorder (p. 168)

Psychogenic pain disorder (p. 168)

Body dysphoric disorder (p. 168)

Hypocondriasis (p. 168)

Conversion disorder (p. 168)

Hysteria (p. 169)

Malingering (p. 170)

La belle indifference (p. 170)

Somatization disorder (p. 170-171)

Social-skills training (p. 178)

Dissociative disorder (p. 179)

Psychogenic amnesia (p. 179)

Psychogenic fugue (p. 179)

Multiple personality (p. 179-182)

STUDY QUESTIONS

SOMATOFORM DISORDERS (p. 168-178)

1. Describe five types of somatoform disorders. (Three of the five are not discussed further.) What do all five types have in common? (p. 168)

2. Give some examples of conversion symptoms involving loss of (a) muscular activity and (b) sensory input.   Describe two problems in diagnosing conversions. (p. 168-170)

3. Describe the somatic complaints and related behaviors which distinguish somatization disorder. (p. 170-173

4. How did the study of conversions lead Freud to important concepts? Summarize Freud's theory of conversions including his later revision of it. (p. 173)

5. How have some contemporary psychoanalysts revised Freud's theory? (p. 173-174)

6. Describe three other theories of conversion disorders.   How well is each supported by research? (p. 174-177)

7. Why has little research been done on the psychological treatment of somatoform disorders?   What is the aim of psychoanalysis and behavioral therapy in treating these disorders?   (p. 177-178)

DISSOCIATIVE DISORDERS (p. 179-186)

8. Define and distinguish among three major dissociative disorders (p. 179-182).   Distinguish between multiple personality and "split personality" as the term is used to describe schizophrenia. (Footnote, p. 180)

9. Summarize the psychoanalytic and learning theory views of dissociative disorders.   Describe research supporting each. (p. 182-185)

10. Describe the traditional therapeutic approach to treating dissociative disorders. Why is hypnosis often used and how effective is it? (p. 185-186)

SELF-TEST, CHAPTER 7

MULTIPLE-CHOICE

1. Which of the following is an example of hypochondriasis?
   a. persistent unsubstantiated fear of having cancer
   b. an ulcer caused by stress
   c. inability to remember being in an auto accident yesterday
   d. recurring pain with no physical basis

2. Conversion disorder is easiest to diagnose when
   a. the symptom does not make anatomical sense.
   b. the person can be shown to be malingering.
   c. the person shows great concern about the seriousness of their symptoms.
   d. a predisposing physical illness can be found.

3. Which is the best label for Ms. Jones, who entertains her friends with delightful stories about her various physical infirmities and her experiences with the medical profession.
   a. conversion disorder
   b. somatization disorder
   c. body dysphoric disorder
   d. hypochondrias

4. Breuer and Freud proposed that conversion disorders were caused by
   a. memories of an earlier traumatic event.
   b. an unconscious reluctance to become an adult.
   c. hallucinations.
   d. repression of an emotionally arousing experience.

5. According to Freud, the primary gain from conversion symptoms is
   a. avoidance of repressed id impulses.
   b. escape from an unpleasant life situation.
   c. obtaining sympathy from a therapist.
   d. the indirect expression of anger.

6. The socio-cultural theory of conversion disorders is supported by the fact that they are more common in which of the following?
    a. close-knit, family oriented cultures
    b. sexually repressive, unsophisticated cultures
    c. primitive cultures with distinctive roles for males and females
    d. cultures whose traditional stories emphasize physical strength and weakness

7. For treating somatization disorder, behavioral clinicians would probably view systematic desensitization as
    a. the ideal treatment.
    b. helpful but insufficient.
    c. inappropriate, since the patient's symptoms do not involve specific fears.
    d. less helpful than cognitive therapy.

8. Psychogenic fugue usually develops
    a. suddenly, without apparent cause.
    b. following a stressful or traumatic event.
    c. in a person with pre-existing autonomic lability.
    d. following a serious physical illness.

9. What is the cause of dissociative disorders according to psychoanalytic theory?
    a. Memories of unacceptable behaviors are repressed.
    b. A direct expression of unconscious aggression.
    c. They allow symbolic expression of repressed urges.
    d. They are a regression to infantile developmental stages.

*10. Research suggests that hypnosis and sodium Amytal
    a. are very effective in helping patients to remember forgotten events.
    b. do not improve memory for forgotten events.
    c. are helpful in getting multiple personalities to "fuse."
    d. may actually create multiple personalities.

SHORT ANSWER

1. Individuals with _____ are preoccupied with imaginary or minor defects in their physical appearance

2. Identify two problems in diagnosing conversion disorders.

3. Psychoanalytic theories suggest that the cause of somatoform disorders is . . .

4. Summarize a behavioral account of the cause of Conversion disorders.

5. How important are genetic and physiological factors in conversion disorders?

6. Why is little known regarding the effectiveness of psychological treatments for somatoform disorders?

7. Summarize the learning model of dissociative reactions?

8. Research on state-dependent memory may help explain dissociative disorders by showing that . . .

9. There has been little research on dissociative disorders because . . .

10. Dissociative disorders (more than other disorders) are commonly treated by psychoanalytic methods because . . .

ANSWERS TO SELF-TEST, CHAPTER 7

MULTIPLE-CHOICE

1. A (p. 168-169)   2. A (p. 169-170)   3. B (p. 171-172)   4. D (p. 173)
5. A (p. 173)   6. B (p. 174-176)   7. B (p. 178)   8. B (p. 179)
9. A (p. 182)   10. B (p. 186)

SHORT ANSWER

1. Body dysmorphic disorder (p. 168)

2. Distinguishing conversion disorders from 1) physical problems and 2) malingering (p. 169-170)

3. Psychological conflicts which are transformed, distorted, or converted into physical form. (p. 173)

4. The individual is acting as he/she believes sick people should act. (p. 176-177)

5. Not very important. Genetic & physiological research has yielded negative or contradictory results (though right-brain, left-brain research suggests interesting speculations.). (p. 177)

6. Because such individuals seek medical rather than psychological treatment. (p. 177-178)

7. Dissociative reactions are seen as avoidance responses or ways of avoiding stressful/unpleasant memories. (p. 182-183)

8. People do not remember as well when in a different emotional state. (p. 184)

9. These states are rare. (p. 185)

10. Psychoanalytic concepts such as unconscious and repression clearly seem applicable. (p. 185)

8. Psychophysiological Disorders

OVERVIEW

This is the third of four chapters on emotional disorders involving stress, and emotionality.

The last two chapters covered psychological disorders that are linked to anxiety. The disorders in Chapter 6 involved more-or-less direct difficulties with anxiety   In Chapter 7 the disorders did not directly involve anxiety but, traditionally, anxiety is suspected to underlie them. These disorders were somatoform disorders (involving physical symptoms) and dissociative disorders (involving memory, consciousness, and identity).

It should, by now, be clear that anxiety is common and is a source of much psychological suffering. Stress and anxiety also have physical effects. Some of these, traditionally called psychophysiological disorders, are discussed in Chapter 8. Heart disease and asthma are examples of these disorders.

After Chapter 8 the next chapter discusses emotional disorders involving affect or feelings; primarily depression. The text then begins Part 3 which deals with Social Problems. Social problems are often not considered disorders or "illnesses" but are of concern to society and/or to the individuals with the problems. Examples of these problems include criminality, substance abuse, and a variety of sexual problems ranging from rape to voyeurism ("Peeping Toms") to impotence.

CHAPTER SUMMARY

Probably all physical illnesses involve psychological factors to some degree. Chapter 8 focuses on physical problems where, traditionally, the involvement has been considered especially strong. The chapter discusses these psychophysiological disorders in general and then discusses some common examples in more detail.

Stress and Health reviews research on stress and it's relation to physical illness in general. *Theories of the Stress-Illness Link:* identifies a number of both physiological and psychological theories regarding this relationship.

Cardiovascular Disorders including hypertension and heart disease appear related to specific styles of responding to stress, especially the suppression of anger.

Asthma attacks involving difficulty in breathing result from combinations of psychological factors and physiological predispositions that vary from individual to individual.

Therapies for Psychophysiological Disorders include both medical treatment of the physical symptoms and psychological methods of controlling the underlying stress. Behavioral medicine, a new specialization, is developing specialized psychological techniques to treat psychophysiological disorders.

ESSENTIAL CONCEPTS

1. Psychophysiological disorders are distinct from conversion reactions involving physical tissue changes that are caused or worsened by emotional factors.

2. There is no listing of psychophysiological disorders in DSM-IIIR because virtually all physical illnesses are now viewed as potentially related to psychological factors.

3. Stress has been difficult to define and measure but a number of research approaches indicate relationships between stress and illness.

4. There are many theories of the link between stress and illness.

5. High blood pressure and coronary heart disease, appear related to Type A behaviors especially the suppression of anger although this research is complex and ongoing.

6. Asthma is another illness apparently resulting from a combination of physical and psychological factors.

7. Where psychological factors contribute to illness, a combination of medical and psychological treatment is needed.

8. Behavioral medicine is developing specific programs for treating psychological factors that contribute to illness.

KEY TERMS

Psychophysiological disorders (p. 190)

Psychosomatic (p. 190)

Dualism & monism (p. 190-191)

Stress (p. 191)

General adaptation syndrome (GAS) (p. 191)

Somatic-weakness theory (p. 197)

Specific reaction theory (p. 197)

Evolution theory (p. 197-198)

Cardiovascular disorders (p. 199)

Essential hypertension (p. 199)

"Anger-in" (p. 200)

Coronary heart disease (p. 202)

Angina pectoris (p. 202)

Myocardial infarction (MI) (p. 202)

Type A behavior (p. 203)

Asthma (p. 206)

Behavioral medicine (p. 211)

Stress management (p. 215-216)

STUDY QUESTIONS

1. Define psychophysiological disorders distinguishing them from conversion disorders (in Chapter 7). How does DSM-IIIR handle psychophysiological disorders and how does this foster a monistic (not dualistic) view? (p. 190-191)

STRESS AND HEALTH (p. 191-197)

2. Describe Selye's and Lazarus' concepts of stress and responses to stress.   (p. 191-192)

3. What is the suspected relationship between stress and illness? Describe two attempts to study this relationship and how the second handles four problems with the first. (p. 192-195)

4. Describe a (moderator) factor illustrating why stress effects people differently.   Describe a (mediator) mechanism illustrating the way stress effects illness. (p. 195-197)

THEORIES OF THE STRESS-ILLNESS LINK (p. 197-199)

5. Briefly summarize five theories of the differential effect stress has on illness. (p. 197-199)

CARDIOVASCULAR DISORDERS (p. 199-207)

6. How important are cardiovascular disorders? Which two cardiovascular disorders are discussed in the text? Define essential hypertension and the course or progression of this condition. (p. 199-200)

7. Describe two groups of studies showing a relation between short-term stress, "anger-in" and increases in blood pressure? Why is it difficult to study long-term factors? What predisposing factor is suggested by research? (p. 200-202)

8. Describe two principal forms of coronary heart disease.   How well do traditional risk factors predict it? (p. 202-203)

9. What is the Type A behavior pattern?   How is it (best) measured and what is it's (probable) relationship to coronary heart disease? (p. 203-205)

10. What physiological and psychological mechanisms relate Type A behavior to heart disease? (p. 205-206)

ASTHMA   (p. 206-211)

11. What happens in an asthma attack.   Describe the general debate
    concerning the etiology of asthma?   What psychological factor can
    produce asthma attacks - at least in some people? (p. 206-209)

12. What has been learned about the following possible contributors to
    asthma: the   role   of   the   family,   personality,   physiological
    predispositions?   (p. 209-211)

THERAPIES FOR PSYCHOPHYSIOLOGICAL DISORDERS (p. 211-217)

13. Describe,   in   general,   the   kind   of   treatments   needed   for
    psychophysiological disorders?   Describe more specific programs in
    the areas of; hypertension, Type A behavior (including societal issues
    involved) and stress management. (p. 211-217)

SELF-TEST, CHAPTER 8

MULTIPLE-CHOICE

1. What is a "monistic" view of human beings?
   a. The human body cannot handle constant change and stress.
   b. Physical and mental processes are inseparable.
   c. Clean living and sexual abstinence promote human health.
   d. Physical illness can be distinguished from psychological problems.

2. Selye defined stress as follows:
   a. an uncontrollable stimulus.
   b. any stimulus that causes an adverse reaction.
   c. a response to environmental conditions.
   d. a response to a psychological perception of threat.

3. What does the Social Readjustment Rating Scale measure?
   a. stressfulness of recent life events
   b. social desirability of stressful adjustments
   c. readjustment following recent illnesses
   d. effects of social prejudice on patients

4. Research suggests that individuals who have many friends with whom they are closely involved are prone to develop
   a. essential hypertension
   b. coronary heart disease
   c. asthma
   d. none of the above - these individuals tolerate stress well

*5. "The crucial factor in the development of asthma is a chronic, unconscious feeling of being smothered by the over-protective mother, which creates difficulty breathing."   Who would be most likely to make this statement?
   a. Hans Selye
   b. Richard Lazarus
   c. Meyer Friedman
   d. Franz Alexander

6. Essential hypertension refers to
   a. anxiety resulting from unavoidable events.
   b. the basic components of stress.
   c. high blood pressure without organic cause.
   d. a pattern of behavior related to heart attacks.

7. What has been suggested as a genetically transmitted diathesis for hypertension in humans?
   a. salt sensitivity
   b. emotional temperament
   c. anger-in
   d. blood pressure reactivity

8. Type A individuals can be described as
   a. defeated, depressed, frustrated
   b. achievement oriented, competitive, impatient
   c. relaxed, feeling in control, enjoying challenge
   d. personable, responsible, outgoing

9. Which disorder appears to be caused by multiple factors whose importance varies widely from individual to individual?
   a. essential hypertension
   b. angina pectoris
   c. myocardial infarction
   d. asthma

10. Mr. and Mrs. Horn's 6-year-old daughter, Emma, has just been diagnosed as having asthma.   What advice would you give the Horns about how to handle Emma now?
    a. They should treat her the same as other children.
    b. They should enter family therapy.
    c. They should live apart from Emma, to avoid provoking a life-threatening asthma attack.
    d. Emma should not be allowed to engage in strenuous activities.

SHORT ANSWER

1. Psychophysiological disorders are not a category in DSM-IIIR because
   . . .

2. Describe the possible physiological link between stress and illness.

3. Summarize the somatic-weakness theory.

4. According to the _____ theory psychophysiological disorders result from differences in the way particular individuals respond physically to stress.

5. How does psychoanalysis account for the fact that people develop different psychophysiological disorders when exposed to the (apparently) same stressors?

6. How important are cardiovascular disorders as a cause of death?

7. Define "essential hypertension".

8. According to research blood pressure may remain low in individuals who respond to stress by . . .

9. Summarize the results of research on the role of personality in causing asthma.

10 What social factors make it difficult to treat Type-A behavior?

ANSWERS TO SELF-TEST, CHAPTER 8

MULTIPLE-CHOICE

1. B (p. 190)   2. C (p. 191) 3. A (p. 192-193) 4. D (p. 195-196)
5. D (p. 198)   6. C (p. 199) 7. D (p. 202)   8. B (p. 203)
9. D (p. 208-209) 10. A (p. 209-210)

SHORT ANSWER

1. Virtually all physical diseases are potentially related to psychological stress (p. 190)

2. Immune system which protects body from physical illness appears to function poorly under stress. (p. 196-197)

3. Disorders will appear in whichever physical system is weakest or most vulnerable to stress. (p. 197)

4. Specific-reaction (p. 197)

5. Unconscious, unresolved, conflicts influence how individuals respond to stress thus producing different disorders. (p. 198)

6. Despite some improvement it remains the leading cause of death in America. (p. 199)

7. High blood pressure with no obvious organic cause. (p. 199)

8. Reacting assertively. Expressing anger in effective, socially acceptable ways. (p. 200)

9. Earlier research suggested asthmatic children were more neurotic but other data suggests the neuroticism may be a result (not cause) of the asthma. (p. 211)

10. Society rewards and encourages Type-A behavior. (p. 214-215)

9. Mood Disorders

OVERVIEW

The previous three chapters have covered a wide range of problems related, in one way or another, to anxiety and stress. Chapter 9 discusses another group of emotionally based disorders - the mood disorders.

So far Chapter 6 has shown that anxiety and stress can lead fairly directly to anxiety disorders. Chapter 7 described how they can lead to symptoms involving sensory and motor loses (somatoform disorders) or involving problems in memory, consciousness, and identity (dissociative disorders). In the psychophysiological disorders, Chapter 8, anxiety and stress produced physical damage and illness

Chapter 9 turns to mood disorders; that is disorders of affect or feelings. By far the most common mood disorder involves a lowered mood - i.e. depression. Some people also experience a heightened mood of elation or mania. This is called a "bipolar disorder" because these people usually swing back and forth between mania and depression.

Like anxiety, sadness and elation are normal experiences for most people from time to time. However, when they become a dominant force in people's lives, they constitute a psychological disorder.

Chapter 9 concludes the text's examination of disorders that are primarily emotional in nature. The next four chapters will be devoted to Social Problems involving behaviors or personality traits that are of concern either to society or to the affected individual. Examples of such problems include criminality, drug abuse, sexual disorders such as rape and incest, and sexual dysfunctions such as impotence and frigidity.

CHAPTER SUMMARY

As reflected in the DSM-IIIR categories, clinicians find that depression may occur alone (unipolar) or may alternate with mania (bipolar). In addition, common practice and DSM-IIIR recognize a difference between major disorders and less serious but chronic disorders. In order to avoid confusion the chapter begins by describing *General Characteristics of Depression and Mania.* It then goes on to present the *Formal Diagnostic Listings* in DSM-IIIR. This approach is slightly different from previous chapters.

Psychological Theories of Depression all propose that depression reflects difficulty in adjusting to loss. Psychoanalytic theory suggests that dependent people remain stuck in sadness because they cannot work through the anger which people also experience following a loss. Beck's cognitive theory suggests that depressives understand events through distortions that lead them to blame themselves for negative outcomes. Seligman suggests that helplessness in controlling negative events leads people to attribute the difficulty to themselves and feel hopeless about influencing outcomes - resulting in depression. More generally research suggest depressed individuals have fewer social supports, perhaps because their behaviors lead others to avoid them.

Psychological Theories of Bipolar Disorder are not well developed. Generally theorists have utilized theories of depression by proposing that mania protects individuals from experiencing their depression.

Physiological Theories of Mood Disorders seem important because of a genetic predisposition, especially for bipolar disorders. Physiological theories suggest that mania and depression reflect difficulty in particular neurotransmitters or particular hormones.

Therapy for Mood Disorders includes psychotherapeutic approaches derived from psychological theories of the causes of depression as well as somatic treatments including electroconvulsive shock and drugs.

Suicide is partially related to depression although many suicidal individuals are not obviously depressed or otherwise disordered. The text reviews basic facts and theories and describes approaches to preventing suicide.

ESSENTIAL CONCEPTS

1. DSM-IIIR lists two major mood disorders (major depression and bipolar disorder) and two chronic mood disorders (dysthymic and cyclothymic disorder).

2. Freud proposed that orally fixated people who experience a loss are unable to accept the anger that results and become depressed.

3. Beck suggests that depression results from logical distortions and argues that depressives have a negative self-schema.

4.   In Seligman's learned helplessness theory of depression uncontrollable negative events lead people to attribute failures to internal, global, stable causes and feel hopeless about changing outcomes.

5. Depressed people have fewer social supports - perhaps because their behaviors lead others to avoid them.

6. There are very few psychological theories of mania. Generally mania is seen as a defense against depression.

7. Genetic data indicate there is a heritable component to major mood disorders, especially bipolar disorder.

8.   Physiological theories suggest problems with certain neurotransmitters or with hormones secreted in the brain.

9. Physiological and psychological theories of depression may be simply two different ways to describe the same phenomenon.

10. Research indicates that Beck's cognitive therapy is the most effective psychological treatment for depression, and, in fact, may be superior to medication.

11. There are a number of effective somatic treatments for depression including electroconvulsive therapy and antidepressant drugs. Lithium is a useful drug in treating bipolar disorder.

12. While all people who commit suicide are not depressed, many people who are depressed think about or attempt taking their own life.

13. Suicide prevention centers have developed methods to help people considering suicide.

KEY TERMS

Depression (p. 220)

Mania (p. 221-222)

Flight of ideas (p. 222)

Major (or unipolar) depression (p. 222)

Bipolar depression(p. 222)

Hypomania (p. 223)

Cyclothymic disorder (p. 224)

Dysthymic disorder (p. 224)

Mourning work (p. 225)

Symbolic loss (p. 225)

Learned helplessness (p. 228)

Attribution (p. 229)

Neurotransmitters (p. 236)

Norepinephrine (p. 236)

Serotonin (p. 236)

Neuroendocrine system (p. 238)

Electroconvulsive therapy (ECT) (p. 241)

Egoistic suicide (p. 245)

Altruistic suicide (p. 245)

Anomic suicide (p. 245)

Suicide prevention centers (p. 248)

Psychological autopsy (p. 248)

STUDY QUESTIONS

GENERAL CHARACTERISTICS OF DEPRESSION AND MANIA (p. 220-222)

1. Give five (at least) different characteristics of depression and mania (p. 220-222)

FORMAL DIAGNOSTIC LISTINGS (p. 222-224)

2. Distinguish between the two major mood disorders (p. 222-223) and the other two mood disorders (p. 224) in DSM-IIIR. What problem remains? (p. 222-224)

PSYCHOLOGICAL THEORIES OF DEPRESSION (p. 224-235)

3. What is the basis of depression according to Freud's psychoanalytic theory and Beck's cognitive theory? Summarize the current status of each theory. (p. 225-227)

4. Describe Seligman's learned helplessness theory of depression and revisions that incorporate the ideas of attribution and hopelessness. What five problems remain? (p. 228-234)

5. Discuss interpersonal aspects of depression by describing the social support networks of depressed individuals and the (possible) reasons for this. (p. 234)

PSYCHOLOGICAL THEORIES OF BIPOLAR DISORDER (p. 235)

6. How have most psychological theories viewed mania? Describe a study suggesting that manics try to conceal low self-esteem. (p. 235)

PHYSIOLOGICAL THEORIES OF MOOD DISORDERS (p. 235-238)

7. Why would evidence of genetic factors strengthen physiological theories of mood disorders? What has been found regarding inheritance of bipolar depression? Of unipolar depression? What possibility does "linkage analysis" suggest? (p. 235-236)

8. What indirect clues and direct studies (two approaches) suggest neurotransmitters linked to mood disorders? (The topic of neurotransmitters was covered in Box 6.5, p. 150-151.) What is the current status of research in this area? (p. 236-238)

9. How has the neuroendocrine system been linked to depression? What do the neurotransmitter and neuroendocrine findings suggest about psychological theories of depression? (p. 238)

THERAPY FOR MOOD DISORDERS (p. 238-242)

10. Describe two psychological therapies for depression and their effectiveness. Identify three more general issues in therapy with depressed individuals. (p. 238-241)

11. Three somatic therapies are described. For each describe, (1) when it is used, (2) how effective it is, and (3) what side effects or problems are common. (p. 241-242)

SUICIDE   (p. 242-249)

12. Do non-depressed people commit suicide? Review and be able to recognize 15 facts about suicide. (Also review some myths about suicide.) (p. 242-244)

13. As an introduction, summarize five points as basic perspectives on suicide. Summarize three formal theoretical perspectives on suicide. (p. 244-246)

14. Why has it been difficult to predict suicide from psychological tests? What have studies suggested about the (a) feelings and (b) cognitive style of suicidal individuals? (p. 246-247)

15. Describe Schneidman's approach to suicide prevention and the more general approach of suicide prevention centers. Describe one method of studying suicide directly. (p. 247-249)

SELF-TEST, CHAPTER 9

MULTIPLE-CHOICE

1. Which of the following is characteristic of depression but not of mania?
   a. lack of interest in daily activities
   b. changes in activity level
   c. sleep problems
   d. reckless behavior

*2. _____ is another term for major depression.
   a. Unipolar disorder
   b. Bipolar disorder
   c. Dysthymic disorder
   d. Cyclothymic disorder

3. In Freud's theory of depression, _____ is the diathesis and _____ is the stress which together lead to depression.
   a. introjection; mourning work
   b. loss; introjection
   c. fixation at the oral stage; loss
   d. the Oedipal complex; repression

4. In Seligman's research, dogs who were exposed to shock which they could not control
   a. were especially quick to learn to avoid shock when escape became possible.
   b. became aggressive and destroyed their cages.
   c. had subsequent difficulty learning to avoid shock.
   d. had convulsions and became immobilized.

5. What was the critical point of recent research on the self-esteem of manic individuals?
   a. They did not overtly admit to low self-esteem.
   b. They showed low self-esteem only when in manic episodes.
   c. Their self-esteem was higher than that of normals.
   d. Their self-esteem matched that of depressed individuals.

6. Which of the following is an obstacle in the path of research on the role of neurotransmitters in depression?
   a. neurotransmitter levels cannot be measured directly in a person's brain.
   b. metabolites of neurotransmitters cannot be measured.
   c. drug therapies have no effect on neurotransmitter levels.
   d. symptoms of disorders other than depression are improved by antidepressant medication.

7. Which of the following has <u>not</u> been shown to be effective in treating depression?
   a. Beck's cognitive therapy
   b. psychoanalysis
   c. tricyclic medication
   d. electroconvulsive shock

8. Electroconvulsive shock therapy has been found to be effective in treating
   a. epilepsy.
   b. schizophrenia.
   c. severe depression.
   d. none of the above.

9. Based on demographic data about suicide in the United States, which of the following people is most likely to commit suicide?
   a. a 15-year-old black male
   b. a 45-year-old black female
   c. a 70-year-old white male
   d. a 30-year-old white female

10. A single man with no friends can no longer bear his loneliness and kills himself. How would this suicide be classified in Durkheim's sociological scheme?
    a. anomic
    b. egoistic
    c. altruistic
    d. intrinsic

SHORT ANSWER

1. List five characteristics of depression in addition to feeling sad.

2. Identify two differences found in affectively disordered individuals which are NOT reflected in the DSM-IIIR labels.

3. What is meant by asking "Are attributions relevant?" in evaluating learned helplessness research?

4. Why do depressed individuals have limited social supports according to research?

5. Most psychological theorists suggest that manic episodes be viewed or interpreted as . . .

6. Neurotransmitter theories of mood disorders originally developed out of research which showed that . . .

7. Describe two strategies used in research on the relationship between neurotransmitters and depression.

8. What do therapists do to treat depression based on cognitive theories of it's cause?

9. The following is an example of Durkheim's _____ suicide
   Joe was a straight-A student who was highly-motivated to become a lawyer. He killed himself after he flunked out of law school his first semester.

10. Describe Schneidman's approach to suicide prevention.

ANSWERS TO SELF-TEST, CHAPTER 9

MULTIPLE-CHOICE

1. A (p. 220-222)   2. A (p. 222)   3. C (p. 225)   4. C (p. 228)
5. A (p. 235)   6. A (p. 237)   7. B (p. 238-239) 8. C (p. 241)
9. C (p. 244)   10. B (p. 245)

SHORT ANSWER

1. Changes in sleep, eating, activity level. Loss of interest, energy, concentration. Negative feelings about self with thoughts of suicide. (p. 220)

2. Severe vs. hypomanic episodes. Presence or absence of psychotic delusions & hallucinations. Presence or absence of melancholic symptoms. (p. 233)

3. Asks if people actually spend much time and energy considering the causes of their behavior? (p. 233)

4. Their interpersonal style is aversive, leads others to reject them. This style precedes depression, thus appears a cause, not a result, of depression. (p. 234)

5. Defenses or attempts to avoid depression. (p. 235)

6. Drugs which relieved depression also increased levels of specific neurotransmitters. (p. 236)

7. 1) Study metabolic by-products of neurotransmitters in the blood, urine, etc. 2) Study whether drugs that effect neurotransmitters also effect the disorders. (p. 237)

8. Help clients identify and change their beliefs using logical analysis, providing contrary examples or experiences, etc. (p. 239-240)

9. Anomic (p. 245)

10. Schneidman emphasizes helping them find & consider other alternatives (also to reduce suffering, reconsider suicide.) (p. 247-248)

10. Personality Disorders and Sociopathy

OVERVIEW

The previous chapter completed the text's discussion of emotional problems. The four chapters in that section studied the problems that arise from anxiety, stress and depression.

Chapter 10 begins four chapters on a cluster of "Social problems". These problems are characterized by particular behaviors or personality traits which are of considerable concern to society and/or to the individual. Generally social problems are not considered "mental illnesses" as the term is commonly used.

Chapter 10 covers personality disorders characterized by persistent personality traits that cause concern. Examples include persistent social withdrawal, self-centeredness, and criminal activity. The remaining chapters cover specific behaviors of social concern. Chapter 11 deals with substance use disorders such as drug and alcohol abuse. Chapters 12 and 13 deal with sexual problems which are divided into sexual disorders or deviations (such as fetishism and rape) and sexual dysfunctions or inadequacies (such as impotence).

After chapter 13 the text will discuss an entirely different kind of problem, schizophrenia, in which individuals are said to be psychotic or "out of contact with reality".

CHAPTER SUMMARY

Personality disorders are defined as inflexible and maladaptive personality traits which impair the individual's functioning. Only one personality disorder is well understood or studied and most of the chapter focuses on this disorder; antisocial personality disorder or sociopathy.

The chapter begins by discussing DSM-IIIR's definition of personality disorders and then defines the *Specific Personality Disorders*.

The classic definition of *Antisocial Personality Disorder (Sociopathy)* emphasizes lack of shame or sense of responsibility.   DSM-IIIR emphasizes their difficulty honoring commitments and maintaining genuine emotional relationships.

Theory and Research on the Etiology of Sociopathy includes several areas.   Research on the families of sociopaths shows they provided inconsistent or little discipline and that fathers themselves were antisocial.   Research also suggests a genetic predisposition to sociopathy.

Several research areas focus on the low anxiety of sociopaths resulting in their inability to inhibit activities that lead to punishment.   Some sociopaths show EEG brain waves suggesting failure of inhibitory processes.   Sociopaths are slow to learn to avoid electric shock but do avoid if artificially aroused.   Physiologically they seem to show little arousal but closer study suggests they anticipate and physiologically tune out stress.

Therapies for Personality Disorders are being developed based on clinical experience.   Psychological and somatic treatment of sociopaths has been unsuccessful.   Prisons remain the common way of handling sociopaths but are used primarily to punish and isolate them.

ESSENTIAL CONCEPTS

1. Personality disorders are characterized by inflexible and maladaptive traits that interfere with functioning.   This Axis II diagnosis is controversial and less reliable than many other diagnostic categories.

2. Antisocial personality disorder or sociopathy is characterized by antisocial behavior involving no sense of responsibility or shame.

3. Evidence suggests that the family plays a role in the development of antisocial behavior in that inconsistent discipline, lack of affection, and parental rejection are predictive of the disorder.

4. Evidence also suggests that genetic factors play a role in etiology of antisocial behavior.

5. Clinical experience and laboratory studies show that the low anxiety of sociopaths inhibits their ability to learn from experience or punishment. They may inhibit or tune out emotional arousal.

6. Ideas for treating personality disorders are evolving out of clinical practice although research is very limited.

7. Attempts at treating antisocial personality disorder have been notably ineffective.

KEY TERMS

Personality disorder (p. 254)

Paranoid personality disorder (p. 254)

Schizoid personality disorder (p. 255)

Schizotypal personality disorder (p. 255)

Borderline personality disorder (p. 256)

Histrionic personality disorder (p. 257)

Narcissistic personality disorder (p. 258)

Avoidant personality disorder (p. 259)

Dependent personality disorder (p. 259)

Obsessive-compulsive personality disorder (p. 259)

Passive-aggressive personality disorder (p. 259)

Antisocial personality disorder (p. 260)

Sociopath, psychopath (p. 260)

Cleckley (p. 263)

Retrospective reports (p. 263)

Positive spikes (p. 267)

Incidental avoidance learning (p. 267)

Underarousal (p. 270)

STUDY QUESTIONS

1. How does DSM-IIIR define personality disorders as a group and why
   are they placed on Axis II?   Briefly identify a practical and a
   theoretical problem with the DSM-IIIR definition.   (p. 254)

SPECIFIC PERSONALITY DISORDERS (p. 254-259)

2. Identify and briefly define eleven personality disorders (including Antisocial Personality Disorder). You will find it helpful to note the three clusters into which they fall. (p. 254-259)

ANTISOCIAL PERSONALITY DISORDER (SOCIOPATHY) (p. 260-263)

3. Describe and compare the definitions of sociopathy offered by Cleckley and DSM-IIIR. Why has it been difficult to conduct research on sociopaths? (p. 262-263)

THEORY AND RESEARCH ON THE ETIOLOGY OF SOCIOPATHY (p. 263-265)

4. What have studies found about the role of the family in sociopathy? (Look for affection, discipline, and father's behavior) (p. 263-264)

5. What did early twin studies suggest about genetic correlates of sociopathic behavior? What do more recent adoptee studies suggest? (p. 264-265)

CENTRAL NERVOUS SYSTEM ACTIVITY AND SOCIOPATHY (p. 265-271)

6. What two abnormalities have been found in the central nervous systems of some sociopaths? (p. 265-267)

7. How have Lykken and others shown, experimentally, the effects of low anxiety on sociopathic behavior? How have later studies shown the role of feedback and attention on this process? (p. 267-270)

8. What are the autonomic manifestations of sociopathic underarousal? Describe two implications of this pattern (Hare's and Quay's). How does this relate to the avoidance learning studies above? (p. 270-271)

THERAPIES FOR PERSONALITY DISORDERS (p. 271-273)

9. How are therapies for personality disorders being developed? As examples, describe two approaches to treating borderline personalities and the general behavioral approach. (p. 271-273)

10. How effective is psychotherapy with sociopaths and why? How effective are prisons in dealing with sociopaths and why? (p. 273)

SELF-TEST, CHAPTER 10

MULTIPLE-CHOICE

1. The personality disorders are based on the _____
   approach to personality.
   a. state
   b. trait
   c. interactive
   d. continuum

2. Most people who have been diagnosed as having a personality
   disorder on DSM-IIIR
   a. have only one personality disorder.
   b. have several Axis I disorders as well.
   c. have more than one personality disorder.
   d. have a learning disability as well.

3. Blake has great difficulty forming relationships with other people.
   He is eccentric looking, wearing dirty and poorly fitting clothing, and
   talks about strange ideas like telepathy, "forces" which other people
   do not experience, and the idea that someone is following him and
   listening to his plans. Which of the following personality disorders
   is the best diagnosis for Blake?
   a. schizotypal
   b. schizoid
   c. paranoid
   d. histrionic

4. What is the primary characteristic of histrionic personality
   disorder?
   a. avoidance of others
   b. multiple, vague physical complaints
   c. dramatic and changeable emotions
   d. inability to make realistic life plans

*5. DSM-III omitted the following important characteristic of
   antisocial personality disorder, later restored in DSM-IIIR:
   a. sadistic tendencies
   b. inability to behave responsibly
   c. lack of remorse
   d. impulsive antisocial acts

6. What has been found in adoptee studies of criminality?
   a. adopted children are more likely to become criminals
   b. biological parents of adopted criminals are more likely to be
      criminals
   c. children are more likely to learn criminal behavior from adoptive
      parents
   d. criminals are more likely to give up children for adoption

7. What has research shown about the brain wave activity of some
   sociopaths?
   a. it is similar to that of young children
   b. rapid, irregular waves predominate
   c. it becomes abnormal when the sociopath is aroused
   d. it is abnormal only in violent sociopaths

8. In Schachter and Latane's (1964) study, sociopaths injected with
   adrenaline were found to
   a. learn to avoid punishment more quickly.
   b. have more difficulty learning to avoid punishment.
   c. respond more aggressively to provocation.
   d. respond less aggressively to provocation.

9. In resting situations, the skin conductance of sociopaths
   a. is lower than normal.
   b. is higher than normal.
   c. is normal.
   d. has not been studied; it is the reactivity that is of interest.

10. Treatment of antisocial personality disorder is very difficult
    because
    a. most clinicians refuse to work with these patients.
    b. such patients are usually unable to form a trusting relationship
       with a therapist.
    c. funding for the disorder is routed to prisons rather than to
       therapeutic efforts.
    d. all of the above.

SHORT ANSWER

1. Define "Personality Disorders" (as a group).

2. Define "Borderline personality disorder".

3. List four classic characteristics of sociopaths in addition to antisocial behavior.

4. Research on the role of the family finds that sociopaths tend to come from families characterized by . . .

5. Why are genetic correlates of sociopathic behavior NOT shown by twin studies which found higher concordances of sociopathy in identical than fraternal twins of sociopaths?

6. How sociopathic "thrill seeking" be understood based on current research?

7. Describe the procedure used to study avoidance learning in sociopaths.

8. How is the "underarousal" view of sociopathy strengthened by results of avoidance learning studies where sociopaths were injected with adrenaline?

9. How are therapies for personality disorders being developed?

10. It can be argued that incarceration is an effective treatment for sociopaths because . . . .

ANSWERS TO SELF-TEST, CHAPTER 10

MULTIPLE-CHOICE

1. B (p. 254)   2. C (p. 254)   3. A (p. 255)   4. C (p. 257-258)
5. C (p. 263)   6. B (p. 264-265)   7. A (p. 265)   8. A (p. 268)
9. A (p. 270)   10. B (p. 273)

SHORT ANSWER

1. Characterized by personality traits which are inflexible, maladaptive and cause impairment or distress. (p. 254)

2. Label for individuals with marked instability in relationships, mood, self-image.. (p. 256)

3. Charming, intelligent, no shame, irresponsible, poor judgment, no lasting friends, no symptoms such as anxiety or delusions, etc. (p. 262-263)

4. Rejection, lack of affection, inconsistent discipline, antisocial fathers. (p. 263-264)

5. Higher concordances among same-sex fraternal twins point to similar child rearing practices (p. 264-265)

6. Research suggests they do not get emotionally aroused easily thus only extreme behavior gives them a thrill. (p. 270-271)

7. Person is asked to learn the correct series of choices and told that punishment will, sometimes, follow errors. Actually punishment follows only one of the possible errors. (p. 267-268)

8. Adrenaline, which increases arousal, improved the avoidance of sociopaths but reduced avoidance of normals (presumably by overarousing them) (p. 268)

9. Being developed based on clinical experiences of therapists (not on scientifically based theory & research). (p. 271-272)

10. They often become less disruptive after middle age. (p. 273)

11. Psychoactive Substance Use Disorders

OVERVIEW

Chapter 11 is the second of four chapters on social problems. These problems involve behavioral or personality patterns that concern society - often more than the individual.

The previous chapter (Chapter 10) covered personality disorders in which persistent personality traits cause concern to either the individual or society. The most obvious personality disorder is the antisocial personality characterized by antisocial behavior and especially by lack of guilt over that behavior.

Chapter 11 will discuss substance abuse disorders including abuse of alcohol, marijuana, nicotine, and hard drugs. Substance abuse problems are particular behaviors rather than general traits like personality disorders but both share the characteristic of being of at least as much concern to society as to the individual with the disorder.

The next two chapters will deal with sexual problems. Chapter 12 discusses sexual disorders or deviant sexual behaviors. Chapter 13 discusses sexual dysfunctions or difficulties in maintaining normal sexual behaviors.

CHAPTER SUMMARY

Drugs have always been used, and abused, to alter mood and consciousness. Contemporary practice distinguishes between substance abuse which effects daily functioning and substance dependence or addiction which produces physiological changes leading to physical tolerance (or decreasing effects) and withdrawal reactions. The chapter discusses the social, psychological, and physical effects of five groups of commonly abused substances.

Alcoholism is a widespread social problem. Alcohol produces short-term effects including poor judgement and coordination and long-term effects including addiction and physical deterioration. A variety of approaches to understanding and treating alcoholism exist.

The so-called hard drugs are illegal, often addictive, drugs and include both *Sedatives* such as narcotics and barbiturates, and *Stimulants* such as amphetamines and cocaine. As with alcoholism, there are a variety of physiological and psychological approaches to understanding and treating abuse of these drugs.

Nicotine and Cigarette Smoking is still common despite increasing evidence of health risks. Recent evidence suggests nicotine is addictive at least when used heavily. There have been many attempts to both prevent and treat nicotine abuse.

Marijuana is commonly used to produce a "high". Stronger forms of marijuana plus increased social usage is producing evidence of physical and, possibly, psychological dangers of long term use. Debate continues over whether it is addictive and over its possible uses in medical treatment. *LSD and Other Psychedelics* were originally studied, and are now abused, for their mind altering properties.

ESSENTIAL CONCEPTS

1. Substance abuse involves abuse of a drug to the extent that in interferes with social, familial,, or occupational functioning.

2. In Substance dependence abuse leads to physiological addiction to the drug evidenced by withdrawal reactions and evidence of increased tolerance.

3. Alcohol is an addicting drug that exacts a high cost from many individuals and from our society.

4. Alcohol's short-term physiological effects are mediated by cognitive expectancies. The long-term consequences can be quite severe both psychologically and physiologically.

5. Sedatives ("downers") reduce the body's responsiveness. They include organic narcotics and synthetic barbiturates.

6. The narcotics (opium and its derivatives, morphine and heroin) are highly addicting and have important social consequences. For example criminal behavior may result from an addict's attempt to maintain the expensive habit.

7. Stimulants (amphetamine and cocaine) are "uppers" that heighten alertness and increase autonomic activity. They are considered addictive.

8. Available treatments for addicts are not particularly successful.

9. Cigarette smoking is a tremendous health problem. Prevention may be the best treatment because it is a very difficult habit to stop. For at least some smokers, it is addicting.

10. Marijuana interferes with cognitive functioning and psychomotor performance and appears to have some adverse physical effects with long-term use.

11. LSD and other psychedelics produce a state that was once thought to mimic psychosis, and is characterized sometimes by dramatic changes in perception and cognition.

KEY TERMS

Polydrug abuse (p. 278)

Psychoactive substance abuse & dependence (p. 279)

Tolerance (p. 279)

Withdrawal symptoms (p. 279)

Alcoholism (p. 279)

Fetal alcohol syndrome (p. 283)

Delirium tremens (DTs) (p. 283)

Delay of reward gradient (p. 286)

Detoxification (p. 289)

Covert sensitization (p. 290)

Controlled drinking (p. 290)

Narcotics (p. 293)

Opium (p. 293)

Morphine (p. 293)

Heroin (p. 293)

Endorphins (p. 294)

Barbiturates (p. 294)

Amphetamines (p. 295)

Cocaine (p. 296)

Heroin substitutes (Methadone) (p. 299-300)

Cross-dependent (p. 300)

Heroin antagonists (p. 300)

Nicotine (p.   302)

Rapid-smoking treatment (p.   306)

Marijuana (& Hashish) (p.   309)

Psychedelics (p.   314)

LSD (p.   314)

Flashbacks (p.   317)

STUDY QUESTIONS

1. Identify and distinguish between two levels of substance use disorders in DSM-IIIR (especially tolerance & withdrawal). Why is polydrug abuse a particular problem? (p.   278-279)

134   Chapter 11

ALCOHOLISM (p. 279-293)

2. How much of a problem is alcoholism from a social and legal point of
   view?   What behaviors distinguish alcohol abuse and alcohol
   dependency? (p. 279-280)

3. What are the short-term and long-term effects of alcohol   (p.   280-
   284)

4. Briefly summarize five theories of alcoholism.   Note that learning
   views and physiological studies each involve three factors. (p.   284-
   288)

5. Briefly describe five treatments for alcoholism.   (Note that most programs combine several of these treatments.)   Identify three more general clinical considerations in treating alcoholism? (p.   289-292)

SEDATIVES AND STIMULANTS (p. 293-302)

6. The text identifies two groups of sedatives and two groups of stimulants.   For each group, describe (1) short-term effects, (2) long-term effects, and (3) withdrawal effects.   (p.   293-298)

7. What physiological and psychological factors that have been suggested in drug addiction. (p. 299)

8. Describe and evaluate four aspects or approaches to treatment of drug abuse. (p. 299-302)

NICOTINE AND CIGARETTE SMOKING (p. 302-309)

9. How common and how serious is cigarette smoking? What evidence suggests that nicotine is addicting, at least for some smokers. (p. 302-304)

10. Describe one specific treatment for smoking.   In general, what is the problem and approach of most treatment programs?   What is the approach of smoking prevention programs. (p.   304-309)

MARIJUANA   (p. 309-314)

11. Describe changes in marijuana use and the reasons for them. Identify three psychological and three somatic effects of marijuana. (p.   309-314)

LSD AND OTHER PSYCHEDELICS (p. 314-318)

12. Summarize the history of LSD and other psychedelics. What are the general effects of psychedelics and what variables influence their effects?   (p.   314-317)

13. What are flashbacks?   Describe a possible psychological explanation for flashbacks. (p.   317-318)

SELF-TEST, CHAPTER 11

MULTIPLE-CHOICE

1. Substance abuse (but NOT dependence) is characterized by
   a. polydrug use
   b. excessive use
   c. increasing tolerance
   d. less severe symptoms

2. Alcohol acts as a _____ on the central nervous system.
   a. stimulant
   b. depressant
   c. narcotic
   d. psychedelic

3. Delirium tremens refers to
   a. the hallucinations common in schizophrenia.
   b. the symptoms that may accompany withdrawal from alcohol.
   c. a symptom of conversion disorder.
   d. the symptoms that accompany an overdose of heroin.

*4. Goodwin et al. (1973) compared adult drinking among those adopted from alcoholic, non-alcoholic but mentally ill, and normal parents. What type of study was this?
   a. epidemiological
   b. experiment
   c. correlational
   d. mixed design

5. Alcoholics Anonymous programs are usually run by
   a. trained paraprofessionals.
   b. psychiatrists or psychologists.
   c. the participants themselves.
   d. mental health professionals who are themselves recovering alcoholics.

6. George is experiencing symptoms similar to a bad flue; he is sneezing, sweating, tearful, yawns frequently, and has muscle pain. Which of the following drugs is he most likely withdrawing from?
   a. cocaine
   b. LSD
   c. amphetamines
   d. heroin

7. The regular use of a low dose of amphetamines in order up late studying abnormal psychology is likely to
   a. be an effective and fairly harmless strategy
   b. induce hostility and paranoia.
   c. cause brain damage.
   d. fail to keep the user awake, because of tolerance effects.

8. Which is characteristic of family backgrounds of drug abusers?
   a. strict discipline
   b. mother uses drugs excessively
   c. antisocial behavior by father
   d. other children favored by parents

*9. The vast majority of smokers who quit do so
   a. through smoking clinics.
   b. with the help of hypnosis.
   c. through rapid-smoking treatment
   d. without professional help.

10. The following is a physiological effect of marijuana use:
   a. lowered sperm count
   b. decreased appetite
   c. insomnia
   d. all of the above

SHORT ANSWER

1. List four indicators of dependence on alcohol.

2. What does the text conclude about descriptions of alcoholic stages such as Jellinek's?

3. The delay of reinforcement gradient is used to explain what in learning theories of alcoholism?

4. Disulfiram or Antabuse can discourage alcoholics from drinking by doing what?

5. According to the best current evidence, can alcoholics learn to drink in moderation?

6. Describe the physiological mechanism apparently responsible for the effects (and withdrawal effects) of opium based drugs.

7. List two abused substances which can have fatal withdrawal side effects.

8. Describe the immediate effects of cocaine.

9. Psychological theories of drug abuse typically seek to explain what?

10. What are the common reasons for use of marijuana?

11. What factors appear responsible for LSD "flashbacks"?

ANSWERS TO SELF-TEST, CHAPTER 11

MULTIPLE-CHOICE

1. D (p. 279)   2. B (p. 280)   3. B (p. 283)   4. C (p. 287-288)
5. C (p. 289-290) 6. D (p. 294)   7. D (p. 295-296) 8. C (p. 299)
9. D (p. 304, 305) 10. A (p. 311-312)

SHORT ANSWER

1. Regular daily drinking, Inability to stop, binges, tolerance, withdrawal symptoms, drinking to relieve withdrawal, etc. (p. 280)

2. Progression of alcoholism is more variable than Jellinek's descriptions imply. (p. 282)

3. Why long-term negative effects of alcohol effect behavior of alcoholics less than short-term positive effects. (p. 286)

4. Produces violent vomiting if individual drinks alcohol after taking it (p. 289)

5. Evidence is controversial but apparently some (only) can do so. (p. 291-292)

6. Drug simulates body's own pain-relieving endorphins but also causes body to decrease production leading to withdrawal effects. (p. 294)

7. Alcohol (p. 283) and barbiturates (p. 295)

8. Reduces pain, heightened sensory awareness, euphoria, sexual desire, self-confidence and energy. (p. 296-298)

9. Why particular kinds of people are especially susceptible to drug abuse. (p. 299)

10. Feelings of being high and relaxed as well as social and political implications. (p. 310)

11. Combination of situations, expectations, and personality patterns encourages sensitivity to non-real experiences which become self-fulfilling. (p. 317)

12. Sexual Disorders: Gender Identity Disorders and the Paraphilias

OVERVIEW

Chapter 12 is the third of four chapters on social problems. Generally these problems are not considered "mental illnesses" as such but involve particular behaviors or personality traits which are of concern to society and/or to the individual. Chapter 10 discussed personality disorders, especially antisocial personality disorders. Antisocial behavior is defined as a "problem" by society not the individual criminal. Chapter 11 discussed substance abuse problems which concern both society and the individual to varying degrees. Social and individual concerns about these problems can change dramatically as has happened with cigarette smoking.

This chapter and the following one will deal with sexual problems. Sexual problems are commonly divided into two groups. This chapter will discuss sexual deviations. As the term implies, sexual deviations refer to sexual activities that society considers deviant or aberrant. Like the personality disorders and substance abuse disorders of the last two chapters, defining a sexual activity as "deviant" involves a social or individual value judgment. Again our social and individual concerns may change as is happening regarding homosexuality.,

Chapter 13 will look at sexual dysfunctions. Sexual dysfunctions are much more common sexual problems involving difficulty in engaging in or enjoying normal sexual functioning. Sexual dysfunctions include premature orgasm, vaginismus, and inhibited sexual desire or arousal. Generally sexual dysfunctions are of most concern to the individual experiencing them.

CHAPTER SUMMARY

Sexual disorders may be divided into three groups. In *Gender Identity Disorders* individuals have a sense of themselves as being of one sex although they are, anatomically, the other sex. Such individuals wish they had the body of the other sex and could live as such. They may seek sex-change surgery to make their physical anatomy consistent with their inner sense of themselves. Behavior therapy can also help them change their behaviors, sexual fantasies, etc. to match their anatomy. Such individuals were often encouraged to dress and act as the opposite sex which suggests the importance of early learning in how we view ourselves sexually.

The Paraphilias involve unusual sexual activities or fantasies which the individual either acts on or is markedly disturbed by. They may involve sexual gratification through intimate articles, cross dressing, or through sexual activities involving pain, children, strangers, etc. Behavior therapists treat such problems using aversion therapy to reduce the unwanted attraction plus social skills training to enable normal sexual relations.

Rape is of particular concern. Many professionals view it as an act of violence rather than a sexual act. It causes much psychological trauma to victims.

Views on *Homosexuality* continue to evolve. It is no longer a DSM label.

ESSENTIAL CONCEPTS

1. Gender identity disorders (transsexualism and gender identity disorder of childhood) involve feeling that one is the opposite of one's anatomical sex.

2. The two major treatments for gender identity disorders -- sex-change surgery and alterations in gender identity -- are quite controversial.

3. Paraphilias involve a deviation in the object of sexual arousal.

4. The more common paraphilias include fetishism, transvestism, incest, pedophilia, voyeurism, exhibitionism, rape, and sadism/masochism.

5. Rape is typically more a crime of aggression and dominance than of sex. It can have a tremendously adverse impact on the victim.

6. Little is known about the specific etiology or the most effective treatments of the paraphilias.

7. Homosexuality is no longer considered an abnormality in DSM-IIIR.

KEY TERMS

Gender identity disorder (p. 323)

Transsexualism (p. 323)

Hermaphroditism (p. 323)

Gender identity disorder of childhood (p. 324)

Sex-change surgery (p. 325)

Paraphilia (p. 330)

Fetishism (p. 330)

Transvestistic fetishism (p. 331)

Incest (p. 332)

Pedophilia (p. 333)

Voyeurism (p. 334)

Exhibitionism (p. 334)

Forcible (& statutory) rape (p. 336)

Sadism and masochism (p. 339-340)

Covert sensitization (p. 342)

Orgasmic reorientation (p. 342)

Ego-dystonic homosexuality (p. 345-346)

STUDY QUESTIONS

GENDER IDENTITY DISORDERS (p. 323-330)

1. Define transsexualism.   Is it explainable as a delusion or as a
   hormonal problem? Explain. (p.   323-324)

2. Define gender identity disorder of childhood.   What appears to be the
   basis for it?   What issue of social values does this raise?   (p. 324-
   325)

3. Describe two therapies for gender identity disorders pointing out problems in evaluating their effectiveness. (p. 325-330)

THE PARAPHILIAS (p. 330-345)

4. What are paraphilias? Distinguish between paraphilias and the unusual sexual urges that most people feel from time to time. (p. 330)

5. Describe seven paraphilias (omitting rape) and note any background or personality factors usually associated with each. Describe the psychoanalytic and learning views of paraphilias (these are described in essentially similar terms for many of the paraphilias.). (p. 330-335 and p. 339-341)

6. Define forcible (as opposed to statutory) rape. What are the effects of rape on victims? (p. 336)

7. What is the motivation of rapists?   What are Brownmiller's views on this topic?   What relationship has been suggested between rape and cultural stereotypes of masculinity and femininity?   (p. 336-338)

8. Describe behavioral approaches to therapy for paraphilias.   Describe three variations or other approaches to treatment. (p. 341-343)

9. Describe two approaches to treating rapists and the effectiveness of each.   Describe the immediate and long-term goals in counseling rape victims. (p. 343-345)

HOMOSEXUALITY (p. 345-348)

10. What position does DSM-IIIR take regarding homosexuality?
    Describe how this evolved and the logical contradiction   of the
    (earlier) DSM-III label.   (p. 345-348)

11. How may future research change as a result of changing views on
    homosexuality. (p. 348)

SELF-TEST, CHAPTER 12

MULTIPLE-CHOICE

1. Jim has felt for as long as he can remember like he is actually a woman trapped in a man's body. He very much wants to have his male sex organs removed and replaced with those of a woman. Jim would be diagnosed as having
   a. gender identity disorder of childhood.
   b. transsexualism.
   c. transvestism.
   d. paraphilia.

2. The definition of which of the following disorders is most influenced by societal values?
   a. transsexualism.
   b. gender identity disorder of childhood.
   c. sexual sadism.
   d. pedophilia.

3. The treatment of a 17-year-old transsexual by Barlow, Reynolds, and Agras (1973) demonstrated that
   a. it is virtually impossible to change the gender identity of a person of that age.
   b. transsexuals who are trained to change their gender identity will usually remain homosexuals.
   c. it is possible to change a person's gender identity, even after puberty.
   d. behavioral interventions are the best treatment for transsexuals.

4. Rick finds women's clothing, particularly undergarments, sexually arousing. He especially enjoys watching his girlfriend undress. Which of the following diagnoses would fit Rick's case?
   a. fetishism
   b. voyeurism
   c. pedophilia
   d. none of the above

5. Most exhibitionists
   a. go on to commit rape.
   b. seek to force physical contact with their victims, but stop short of rape.
   c. seek to persuade the woman to have physical contact, without using force.
   d. do not seek physical contact with their victims.

6. Statutory rape refers to
   a. sexual intercourse between a man and any girl under the age of 18.
   b. father-daughter incest.
   c. rape between a husband and wife.
   d. "date rape."

7. One theoretical understanding of rape is based on which of the following ideas?
   a. stereotypes of masculinity and femininity
   b. sexual repression in modern society
   c. hormonal drives of young males
   d. parallels to the pain of child birth

8. Orgasmic reorientation involves
   a. punishing the patient with an unpleasant stimulus while he is having an orgasmic response to unconventional fantasy.
   b. pairing orgasm with conventional sexual stimuli.
   c. using a sexual surrogate to help the patient reach orgasm in a more conventional manner.
   d. teaching transsexuals how to achieve orgasm after a sex-change operation.

9. Why might castration be ineffective in preventing rape?
   a. It is illegal to enforce castration, even on criminals.
   b. Castration does not improve the poor social skills of the rapist.
   c. A castrated man can still commit violent sexual assault.
   d. Castration is, in fact, an effective means of preventing rape, though it is abhorrent to many people and so is not widely used.

10. In DSM-IIIR when would a person be labeled homosexual?
    a. when homosexuality becomes a predominant sexual outlet
    b. when the individual is unable to experience heterosexual arousal
    c. when the individual is disturbed by his/her sexual orientation
    d. never, there is no such label

SHORT ANSWER

1. Define gender identity disorder.

2. Describe in general the psychological procedures used to treat gender identity disorders.

3. Define paraphilias in general

4. What is the cause of many paraphilias according to learning theories?

5. What are the psychological effects of rape on the victim?

6. What is the typical motivation of rapists?

7. Describe procedures commonly used in treating paraphilias.

8. Psychological treatment for paraphilias is complicated by the fact that . . .

9. Identify at least three goals of therapy for rape victims.

10. How may research change as a result of changing views on homosexuality?

ANSWERS TO SELF-TEST, CHAPTER 12

MULTIPLE-CHOICE
1. B (p. 323)   2. B (p. 324-325) 3. C (p. 329-330)   4. D (p. 331)
5. D (p. 335)   6. A (p. 336)   7. A (p. 338)   8. B (p. 342)
9. C (p. 343)   10. D (p. 345)

SHORT ANSWER
1. Label describing people who inwardly feel or believe themselves the opposite sex than they are anatomically. (p. 323)

2. Behavioral methods used to shape specific behaviors and sexual arousal patterns. (p. 327-328)

3. Label for people who are attracted to deviant (unusual or unacceptable) sexual activities.   The attraction must be intense & recurrent so that the individual has acted on them or is markedly distressed by them. (p. 330)

4. The object or activity has come to be paired with sexual arousal through classical conditioning. (p. 331-335)

5. Terrified & violated during attack.   Afterwards tense, humiliated, angry or guilty.   Nightmares, continued fears, sexual difficulties common. (p. 336)

6. Anger, aggression toward females, etc.   Sex is often part of the motivation but not the exclusive or major motivator. (p. 336-337)

7. Behavioral procedures tailored to individual but often using aversive procedures to decrease inappropriate attractions and procedures to condition appropriate attractions and teach social skills. (p 341-343)

8. Individuals engage in these behaviors for many reasons. (p. 342)

9. Help with immediate emotional crisis, legal and medical procedures. Afterwards help deal with feelings about attack, relations with other males and their reactions. (p. 343-344)

10. Focus on changing social prejudices against homosexuality and helping homosexuals cope with these prejudices.   Also on psychological factors in sexuality more generally. (p. 348)

13. Sexual Dysfunctions

OVERVIEW

This is the last of four chapters devoted to social problems. So far, the chapters have covered a wide range of behaviors and lifestyles which are not normally considered "mental illnesses" but which are objectionable to society or to the individual. Chapter 10 described personality disorders especially antisocial personality disorders characterized by lack of guilt. Chapter 11 covered substance abuse.

Chapters 12 and 13 deal with sexual problems. Chapter 12 focused on sexual disorders involving socially objectionable sexual behaviors. In many cases the individuals involved share society's disapproval of the behaviors but engage in them anyway.

Chapter 13 will discuss sexual dysfunctions in which people wish to enjoy normal sexual activities but are inhibited in doing so. Like sexual disorders (in Chapter 12) sexual dysfunctions involve specific sexual behaviors. They differ in that they are typically problems for the individual experiencing the dysfunction rather than problems of social concern. Sexual dysfunctions limit the sufferer's ability to participate fully in intimate relations. They result in frustrations and misunderstandings that can destroy the most rewarding of relations.

Chapter 13 finishes the text's discussion of social problems. Chapter 14 will discuss schizophrenia. The bizarre, disorganized behaviors of schizophrenics have been the source of much research and theoretical interest over the years. Despite this effort, our knowledge of the causes and treatment of schizophrenia remains distinctly limited. In fact, disagreement continues even over how to describe and understand the problem.

CHAPTER SUMMARY

Sexual Disorders and the Human Sexual Response Cycle describes sexual dysfunctions as disruptions or inhibitions in one of the four stages of human sexual responding. Most people experience these disruptions from time to time.   The disruptions are considered sexual dysfunctions only if they   are persistent, recurrent problems.

The Sexual Dysfunctions: Descriptions and Causes describes nine dysfunctions.   While organic factors may be involved, psychological factors are usually central.   *Theories of Sexual Dysfunctions* summarizes the general view, developed by Masters and Johnson, that historical factors, such as early sexual teachings and experiences, may lead the individual to develop performance fears or adopt a spectator role thus inhibiting full participation in sexual activities.   Other contemporary views suggest additional factors.

Behavioral and Cognitve Therapies for Sexual Dysfunctions focus both on sexual skills and on the relationship.   Methods include providing information, exploring attitudes, and providing new sexual skills and experiences.   Medical procedures are included where appropriate. Research results suggest that these procedures are quite effective in relieving the suffering of most individuals with sexual dysfunctions.

ESSENTIAL CONCEPTS

1. Sexual dysfunctions are inhibitions or disturbances in one of four phases of the human sexual response cycle

2. The sexual response cycle is described as having appetitive, excitement, orgasm, and resolution phases.

3. Sexual dysfunctions include; (in the appetitive phase) hypoactive sexual desire and sexual aversion, (in the excitement phase) female arousal and male erectile disorders, (in the orgasm phase) inhibited female or male orgasm and premature ejaculation, as well as sexual pain disorders of vaginismus, and dyspareunia.

4. The general theory of dysfunctions (adapted from Masters and Johnson) is that historical factors (including religious orthodoxy, psychosexual trauma, inadequate education, and physiological causes) lead to current factors (performance fears and the spectator role) resulting in sexual dysfunctions.

5. Other contemporary views have suggested additional factors in the development of sexual dysfunctions.

6. Behavioral and cognitive treatments for sexual dysfunctions are very effective. They include anxiety reduction, education, frank discussion about sexuality, and specific techniques for treating dysfunctions.

KEY TERMS

Sexual dysfunctions (p. 352)

Sexual response cycle (p. 352)

Hypoactive sexual desire disorder (p. 356)

Sexual aversion disorder (p. 356)

Female sexual arousal disorder (p. 356)

Male erectile disorder (p. 356)

Inhibited female orgasm (p. 357)

Inhibited male orgasm (p. 358)

Premature ejaculation (p. 358)

Dyspareunia (p. 359)

Vaginismus (p. 359)

Spectator role (p. 361)

Fears of performance (p. 361)

In vivo desensitization (p. 370)

Sensory-awareness procedures (p. 370)

STUDY QUESTIONS

1. Distinguish between "sexual dysfunctions" and the "sexual disorders" discussed in the previous chapter. Why are dysfunctions difficult for both the individual and his/her relationships?   (p. 352)

SEXUAL DISORDERS AND THE HUMAN SEXUAL RESPONSE CYCLE (p. 352-353)

2. Describe four phases of the human sexual response cycle and their relation to the four categories of sexual dysfunctions in DSM-IIIR. (p. 352-353)

THE SEXUAL DYSFUNCTIONS: DESCRIPTIONS AND CAUSES (p. 353-359)

3. At what point should people begin to think of themselves as being sexually dysfunctional? Why should you be cautious about believing everything the text will say about causes of dysfunctions? (p. 353-356)

4. The text describes a total of nine dysfunctions under four categories. For each, summarize, (1) the definition, (2) any problems with the definition, and (3) possible causes of the problem. (p. 356-359)

THEORIES OF SEXUAL DYSFUNCTIONS (p. 359-367)

5. According to Masters and Johnson, how do current and historical factors interact to result in sexual dysfunctions?   Briefly describe their two current and eight historical factors. (p. 359-363)

6. Summarize seven additional factors suggested by other contemporary work on sexual dysfunctions. (p. 363-367)

BEHAVIORAL AND COGNITIVE THERAPIES FOR SEXUAL DYSFUNCTIONS (p. 367-371)

7. In general, how effective are behavioral and cognitive therapies for sexual dysfunctions? (p. 367-369)

8. Briefly describe nine techniques used in treating sexual
   dysfunctions.   Notice that, in practice, combinations of these
   techniques are used. (p. 370-371)

SELF-TEST, CHAPTER 13

MULTIPLE-CHOICE

1. Sexual dysfunctions (but <u>not</u> sexual disorders) can be described as
   a. having little effect on others.
   b. indicators of underlying psychological disorders.
   c. inhibitions in normal sexual responses.
   d. unusual in the normal population.

2. Premature ejaculation is a disorder of the _____ phase
   of the sexual response cycle.
   a. appetitive
   b. excitement
   c. orgasm
   d. resolution

3. When should people consider themselves as having a sexual
   dysfunction?
   a. when the problem first manifests itself
   b. when the problem becomes common
   c. when the problem occurs with several partners
   d. when the problem starts to affect their relationships

*4. The following DSM-IIIR diagnosis used to be called "impotence":
   a. sexual aversion disorder
   b. male erectile disorder
   c. inhibited male orgasm
   d. dyspareunia

5. Women who never have orgasms usually
   a. have lowered sexual desire.
   b. do become aroused during lovemaking.
   c. have an arousal disorder.
   d. experience pain during intercourse.

6. Which dysfunction is most commonly caused by medical problems?
   a. female sexual arousal disorder
   b. male erectile disorder
   c. premature ejaculation
   d. dyspareunia

7. Which of the following is a historical antecedent leading to sexual dysfunctions according to Masters & Johnson?
a. excessive intake of alcohol
b. anxiety about pleasing partner
c. belief that one should have an orgasm
d. deeply seated psychological problems

8. According to research findings, anxiety is probably more important in the _____ of sexual dysfunctions than in their

_____.
a. historical causes; current causes
b. etiology; maintenance
c. understanding; treatment
d. maintenance; initial causes

9. Directed masturbation is primarily used as a treatment for
a. inhibited female orgasm
b. inhibited male orgasm
c. vaginismus
d. dyspareunia

*10. In sex therapy, psychodynamic techniques
a. are of little or no value.
b. are most useful when clients have difficulty verbalizing their sexual difficulties.
c. are most useful for clients who do not have a current partner with whom to practice behavioral techniques.
d. are an essential part of treatment of most sexual dysfunctions.

SHORT ANSWER

1. List, in order, the four stages of the sexual response cycle as described by current theorists.

*2. Most modern sexologists agree that female orgasms are evoked by stimulation of _____.

3. Why should you be cautious about believing everything the text says about causes of sexual dysfunctions?

4. Why has it been difficult to adequately define premature ejaculation?

5. Define "functional vaginismus".

6. Inhibited female orgasm has been attributed to what causes?

7. Describe the two current factors involved in sexual dysfunctions according to Masters & Johnson.

8. Why do current factors make sexual intercourse and enjoyment difficult?

9. List a number of components of therapy for sexual dysfunctions which do NOT focus directly on sexual activity as such.

*10. Describe "sensate focusing" as a component of sexual therapy.

ANSWERS TO SELF-TEST, CHAPTER 13

MULTIPLE-CHOICE

1. C (p. 352)   2. C (p. 353, 358) 3. B (p. 352)   4. B (p. 356)
5. B (p. 358)   6. D (p. 359)   7. A (p. 362)   8. D (p. 367)
9. A (p. 370)   10. B (p. 370-371)

SHORT ANSWER

1. Excitement phase, Plateau phase, Orgasmic phase, Resolution phase. (p. 353)

2. The clitoris. (p. 354)

3. Much current knowledge is based on reports & interpretations of clinicians working with dysfunctional people. There has been little formal research. (p. 356)

4. Hard to decide when ejaculation is too fast. Should it be defined by time, by satisfying partner, by satisfying individual? (p. 358)

5. Involuntary contractions of the vagina when insertion is attempted. (p. 359)

6. Lack of experience, or poor knowledge of one's own sexual responses, social inhibitions, poor communication, fear of losing control, relationship problems. (p. 358)

7. Fears of performance (fear one won't satisfy self or partner) and the spectator role (excessive thinking about what's happening). (p. 361)

8. They distract or divert the individual's attention away from sexual stimulation & enjoyment. (p. 361)

9. Sex education, anxiety reduction, skills & communication training, Shifts in routine, marital & other therapy, etc. (p. 370-371)

10. Couple undress and practice giving (and receiving) pleasure by touching and caressing each other. (p. 368)

14. Schizophrenia

OVERVIEW

Chapter 13 discussed sexual dysfunctions and was the last of four chapters on social problems.

Chapter 14 discusses schizophrenia. Of all the disorders covered in the text, schizophrenia comes closest to the common understanding of "madness" or "insanity". Despite extensive study, it remains a major concern both socially and scientifically. Historically, psychologists have disagreed on how to define schizophrenia and even on whether the term refers to one or to several different problems. Despite recent advances, no cure for schizophrenia has yet emerged. Schizophrenics constitute a major portion of mental hospital and clinic patients.

After Chapter 14 the next section of the text deals with developmental disorders. Developmental disorders cover the range of problems people may develop in the processes of growing up, facing adulthood, and growing old. These disorders include problems often first seen in children, including mental retardation.

CHAPTER SUMMARY

The History of the Concept of schizophrenia has included two traditions. Many American ideas about schizophrenia developed out of Bleuler's broad, psychoanalytically based, definition. DSM-IIIR has moved toward Kraepelin's narrower, descriptive (rather than theoretical), approach which has been popular in Europe.

Clinical Symptoms of Schizophrenia are divided into five areas. Thought problems include both the content or ideas expressed such as delusions and the form or manner in which schizophrenics think. Disorders of perception and attention are manifested in hallucinations or distorted sensory experiences. Peculiar motor and affective symptoms, as well as distinctive impairments in life functioning are common.

DSM-IIIR recognizes three *Subcategories of Schizophrenia.* Disorganized schizophrenics exhibit blatantly bizarre and silly behaviors. Catatonic schizophrenics show primarily motor symptoms including wild excitement and apathetic withdrawal to the point of immobility. Paranoid schizophrenics have organized delusions of persecution, grandiosity, and jealousy. Other ways of subcategorizing schizophrenics have also developed.

Research on the Etiology of Schizophrenia has been extensive. Genetic, biochemical and neurological data strongly suggest a physiological diathesis to schizophrenia.

Genetic data from family, twin, and more sophisticated adoptee studies all point to a genetic predisposition to schizophrenia. Biochemical research suggests excessive activity in nerve tracts of the brain that utilize the neurotransmitter dopamine for some schizophrenics. New neurological techniques suggest brain atrophy in other schizophrenics leading to speculation that different physiological factors may be involved for these individuals.

Other research has looked at social class, family and other variables. Since schizophrenia runs in families it possible to select and follow children with a high risk of becoming schizophrenic. These studies suggest additional factors.

Many physical and psychological *Therapies for Schizophrenia* have been attempted. Antipsychotic drugs were a major advance. However schizophrenics need additional help to cope with social living. Traditional psychotherapeutic approaches have not been very effective with schizophrenics but family and behavioral methods show promise. There remains a need to integrate our best understandings in order to help schizophrenics lead as normal a life as possible.

ESSENTIAL CONCEPTS

1. Historically definitions of schizophrenia have varied including Kraepelin's dementia praecox and Bleuler's loose associative threads concepts.

2. The major symptoms of schizophrenia are disordered thought, disorders of perception and attention, motor behavior, affective abnormalities, and problems in life functioning.

3. The three major subcategories of schizophrenia are disorganized, catatonic, and paranoid.

4. A new distinction is being made between positive symptoms (hallucinations, delusions, bizarre behavior) and negative symptoms (flat affect, language deficits, apathy, anhedonia, and attentional impairment).

5. Evidence from family, twin, and adoption studies indicates that a substantial genetic diathesis to schizophrenia, although genetics cannot fully explain the disorder's etiology.

6. Recent evidence suggests that excess dopamine activity and brain pathology appear to be related to symptoms in different subsets of schizophrenic patients.

7. There is a link between low social status and schizophrenia. Social drift and social stress explanations this correlation have been offered.

8. There is little strong evidence that the family plays an important etiological role in schizophrenia, although recent data suggest that family emotional expression may effect the adjustment of schizophrenics.

9. Children of schizophrenic patients are being studied longitudinally in a number of high-risk projects which may shed light on the etiology of schizophrenia.

10. Neuroleptic medications are generally quite effective in controlling the more dramatic symptoms of schizophrenia.

11. There is little evidence that traditional psychotherapy is an effective treatment for schizophrenia.

12. Family therapy and behavioral approaches show promise in improving the social adjustment of schizophrenics.

13. There remains a need to integrate our best understandings to better help schizophrenics.

KEY TERMS

Schizophrenia (p. 376)

Dementia praecox (p. 376)

Process-reactive   (p. 378)

Thought disorder (p. 379-380)

Incoherence (p. 380)

Neologism (p. 380)

Loose associations (p. 380)

Delusions (p. 380)

Hallucinations (p. 382)

Catatonic immobility (p. 383)

Waxy flexibility (p. 383)

Flat affect (p. 383)

Inappropriate affect (p. 383)

Disorganized (or hebephrenic) schizophrenia (p. 385)

Catatonic schizophrenia (p. 386)

Paranoid schizophrenia (p. 386)

Grandiose delusions (p. 386)

Delusional jealousy (p. 386)

Ideas of reference (p. 386)

Undifferentiated schizophrenia (p. 386)

Residual schizophrenia (p: 386)

Positive & negative symptoms (p. 386)

Phenothiazines (p. 392)

Excess dopamine activity (p. 393)

Sociogenic hypothesis (p. 396)

Social-drift theory (p. 396)

Schizophrenogenic mother (p. 396)

Double bind hypothesis (p. 396)

Insulin coma therapy (p. 360

Prefrontal lobotomy (p. 399)

Neuroleptics (p. 400)

Direct analysis (p. 403)

STUDY QUESTIONS

HISTORY OF THE CONCEPT (p. 376-379)

1. Describe Kraepelin's and Bleuler's early views on schizophrenia. Trace the way Bleuler's broader view developed in America. (p. 376-379)

2. List four ways in which the new DSM definitions of schizophrenia have moved toward the narrower European view. (p. 379)

CLINICAL SYMPTOMS OF SCHIZOPHRENIA (p. 379-384)

3. Summarize the symptoms of schizophrenics in five areas (with sub areas). Be able to describe symptoms of each using appropriate terms. (p. 379-384)

SUBCATAGORIES OF SCHIZOPHRENIA (p. 384-387)

4. Summarize one or two distinguishing characteristics of each of the three subcategories of schizophrenia in DSM-IIIR. (p. 384-386)

5. Briefly explain the limitations of the DSM-IIIR subcategories. Briefly describe another approach to subcategorizing schizophrenia. (p. 386-387)

RESEARCH ON THE ETIOLOGY OF SCHIZOPHRENIA (p. 387-394)

6. Summarize the results and criticisms of three approaches to studying genetic factors in schizophrenia. How important are genetic factors? How does a diathesis-stress model describe these results? (p. 387-392)

7. Why have biochemical factors in schizophrenia been hard to study? Summarize findings regarding excess dopamine activity as a factor in schizophrenia (seven in all, either supportive or critical). (p. 392-394)

8. Summarize two recent neurological findings concerning
schizophrenia. What sub-group of schizophrenics appear to have
neurological damage and and what sub-group may have excess
dopamine activity (p. 394-395) (You may find it helpful to review
Study Question #5 above.)

9. What relationship has been found between social class and
schizophrenia? Summarize a study which may resolve the two
theories about this relationship. (p. 395-396)

10. Briefly describe two early views on the role of the family; i.e. the
schizophrenogenic mother and the double-bind. What does more
recent research suggest about role of the family in causing or
maintaining schizophrenia? (p. 396-398)

11. How are high-risk studies used to study schizophrenia? (p. 398-399)

THERAPIES FOR SCHIZOPHRENIA (p. 399-407)

12. Why were earlier somatic treatments abandoned?   What are the benefits and the problems with neuroleptic drugs?   What is the current view regarding their use?   (p. 399-401)

13. Identify four psychological approaches to treatment of schizophrenics. For each describe, a) the goal, b) the method and, c) the results. (Two methods for Freudian insight and family therapy approaches) (p. 401-406)

14. What view of schizophrenia is emerging and what three general trends in treatment may develop out of this view? (p. 406)

15. Give four reasons why integration of somatic and psychological interventions is needed? What general problem in the field threatens integration efforts? (p. 406-407)

SELF-TEST, CHAPTER 14

MULTIPLE-CHOICE

1. Kraepelin's term, dementia praecox, reflects his idea of the following core characteristics of the disorder:
   a. intellectual decline and religious delusions
   b. hallucinations and mood fluctuations
   c. stereotyped behavior and autistic aloneness
   d. intellectual decline and early onset

2. Which of the following is not part of the newer DSM-IIIR definition of schizophrenia?
   a. symptoms for at least six months
   b. biochemical confirmation
   c. affective symptoms excluded
   d. mild forms excluded

3. Which of the following is an example of a disorder of thought form in schizophrenia?
   a. incoherence
   b. delusions
   c. "made" volitional acts
   d. thought broadcast

4. In catatonic schizophrenia, which of the following symptom areas is most obviously disturbed?
   a. thought form
   b. attention and perception
   c. affect
   d. motor functions

5. If genetic transmission was the only factor in the etiology of schizophrenia, the concordance of the disorder for monozygotic twins would be
   a. 100%
   b. 80%
   c. 50%
   d. 0%

6. Which of the following drugs is most likely to cause a state similar to paranoid schizophrenia and exacerbate symptoms when taken by a schizophrenic?
   a. LSD
   b. barbiturates
   c. heroin
   d. amphetamines

7. What group of schizophrenics are most likely to show neurological damage?
   a. those with negative symptoms
   b. those with catatonic symptoms
   c. those with excess dopamine activity
   d. those from lower socioeconomic backgrounds

8. Which of the following (hypothetical) findings supports the sociogenic theory of the relationship between social class and schizophrenia?
   a. Most schizophrenics are in a lower social class than their fathers.
   b. Most schizophrenics are in a higher social class than their fathers.
   c. Fathers of schizophrenics are most often from the lowest social class.
   d. Fathers of schizophrenics are most often from the highest social class.

9. A "schizophrenogenic mother" has been described as
   a. bizarre and thought-disordered.
   b. cold and conflict-inducing.
   c. warm and smothering.
   d. all of the above

10. What is the current view on the use of neuroleptic drugs to control schizophrenia?
   a. They have been largely discontinued.
   b. They are widely used in conjunction with other treatments only during hospitalization.
   c. They are a primary treatment despite side-effects.
   d. They are used where other treatments have failed.

SHORT ANSWER

1. What characteristics of the problem were emphasized by A) Kraepelin's term "dementia praecox" and B) Bleuler's term "schizophrenia"?

2. Acceptance of Bleuler's ideas about schizophrenia in America led to what result?

3. What characteristic of schizophrenic speech is illustrated by each of the following.
   A. "I feel fine, on the line, just my kind."

   B. "I'm all frammeled out with psychobabbelology."

   C. "His pants were blue as the sky with clouds floating across it, all fluffy like pink cotton candy that tastes like strawberries."

4. A "delusion" is a _____ while a hallucination is a _____

5. Why is there much interest in positive and negative symptoms of schizophrenia?

6. Briefly discuss the importance of genetic factors in the development of schizophrenia.

7. In what way does the effect of phenothiazines suggest that dopamine is involved in schizophrenia?

8. What view of schizophrenia is emerging currently?

9. Describe the research procedures used in "high-risk" studies of
   schizophrenia.

10. In treating schizophrenia why is integration of somatic and
    psychological interventions needed?

ANSWERS TO SELF-TEST, CHAPTER 14

MULTIPLE-CHOICE

1. D (p. 376)   2. B (p. 379)   3. A (p. 380)   4. D (p. 386)
5. A (p. 392)   6. D (p. 394)   7. A (p. 394-395)   8. C (p. 396)
9. B (p. 396)   10. C (p. 400-401)

SHORT ANSWER

1. A) Early onset and progressive intellectual deterioration B) Underlying difficulty in efficient thinking & communication. (p. 376-377)

2. Gradually the definition broadened until people with widely differing symptoms all came to be labeled schizophrenic. (p. 378-379)

3. A) Clang associations. B) neologisms. C) Loose associations. (p. 380)

4. Distorted thought, distorted perception. (p. 381, 382)

5. It suggests two types of schizophrenia (p. 386) that may have different causes (p. 395)

6. Although earlier studies were flawed, recent studies suggest that genetic factors predispose individuals to develop schizophrenia under certain conditions.   (p. 392)

7. Phenothiazines, which alleviate schizophrenic symptoms, produce side effects resembling Parkinson's which is caused by low dopamine. They also control amphetamine psychoses. (p. 393-394)

8. Emerging view that both genetic predisposition and stress are involved. (p. 406)

9. Children of schizophrenic mothers are intensively studied as they grow up. Later those who develop schizophrenia are compared to those who do not. (p. 398-399)

10. Both approaches have limitations which can be overcome by the other approach. (p. 406-407)

15. Emotional and Behavioral Disorders of Childhood and Adolescence

OVERVIEW

Chapter 14 completed the discussion of schizophrenia.

Chapter 15 begins three chapters covering developmental disorders. These include not only problems of childhood and growing up but also problems of the elderly and growing old. In some cases these disorders are specifically linked to developmental variables. In others, the disorders are usually first noticed at certain ages and the causes are more varied or are unknown.

Chapter 15 deals with childhood disorders that are fundamentally emotional and behavioral in nature. Childhood disorders involving cognitive and intellectual functions are covered in Chapter 16. Chapter 17 concludes the section by discussing problems of the elderly. The chapters cover a wide variety of disorders reflecting increasing understanding of these special age groups.

CHAPTER SUMMARY

The section on *Classification* points out that professionals, and DSM-IIIR, are realizing that children develop a wide range of problems including many which cannot be understood as simple extensions of adult problems. The chapter is organized around three kinds of problems.

Disorders of Undercontrolled Behavior include attention-deficit hyperactivity disorder and conduct disorders. Children with attention-deficit hyperactivity disorder have trouble focusing their attention leading to difficulty in school and play activities. Conduct disorders involve acting out behaviors such as juvenile delinquency. Both have been attributed to a wide variety of factors including physiological or genetic deficits and family upbringing.

In *Disorders of Overcontrolled Behavior*, fears and worries lead to problems such as school phobia, withdrawal and depression. School phobia may be better thought of as fear of separation from parents. Other overcontrol problems are often not recognized and are poorly understood. Treatment often involves encouraging contact with what is feared and family therapy.

Two *Eating Disorders* are recognized. Anorexia nervosa involves inadequate food intake so that the victim, usually female, may starve to death. Bulimia nervosa, in which the individual gorges herself then purges the food by vomiting or using laxatives is less life-threatening but can also have serious physical consequences. Neither is well understood. Treatment may involve hospitalization to stabilize food intake followed by family or other therapy.

ESSENTIAL CONCEPTS

1. Childhood disorders are poorly understood compared to adult disorders. Recent editions of DSM include more detailed listing of childhood disorders than previously.

2. Overcontrol and undercontrol are two broad dimensions of childhood disorders that are consistently identified.

3. Disorders of undercontrolled behavior include hyperactivity and conduct disorders.

4. Attention-deficit hyperactivity disorder probably has multiple causes and is characterized by inattention, impulsivity, overactivity, academic difficulties, and troubled peer relationships.

5. Conduct disorders are difficult to distinguish from normal childhood misbehaviors. They tend to be long-lasting difficulties that resist treatment.

6. Overcontrolled behavior disorders (e.g. fears, social withdrawal, and depression) are frequently overlooked by adults.

7. Childhood fears are often treated by encouraging contact with the feared stimulus.

8. Anorexia nervosa (a dramatic,often life-threatening, loss of weight) and bulimia (binge-eating and self-induced vomiting), are poorly understood and difficult to treat.

KEY TERMS

Disorders of undercontrolled behavior (p. 413)

Attention-deficit hyperactivity disorder (p. 413)

Conduct disorders (p. 419)

Conduct disorder-group type
  and -solitary aggressive type (p. 419)

Coercion hypothesis (p. 423)

Disorders of overcontrolled behavior (p. 425)

School phobia (p. 426)

Social withdrawal disorder (p. 429)

Elective mutism (p. 429)

Anorexia nervosa (p. 431)

Bulimia nervosa (p. 433)

STUDY QUESTIONS

CLASSIFICATION (p. 412-413)

1. How and why has the approach to classifying childhood problems changed over the years? Why is it important to remember that problem children are identified by others, not themselves? (p. 412-143)

DISORDERS OF UNDERCONTROLLED BEHAVIOR (p. 413-425)

2. What are the characteristics of attention-deficit hyperactivity disorder (ADHD)? Why is it difficult to distinguish between ADHD, conduct disorders and "just an active kid". (p. 413-417)

3. Why is no one theory likely to explain all hyperactivity? Briefly list and evaluate six theories of hyperactivity. (p. 417-418)

4. Briefly list and evaluate three treatments for hyperactivity. (p. 418-419)

5. Describe two types of conduct disorders. Why is it difficult to decide when to apply these labels? (p. 419-421)

6. What evidence exists for physiological explanations of conduct disorders? Summarize the psychological theories pointing out how they are similar. (p. 421-423)

7. Why is treatment of conduct disorders important - and difficult? Describe and evaluate two approaches. (p. 423-425)

DISORDERS OF OVERCONTROLLED BEHAVIOR (p. 425-431)

8. Describe childhood fears, school phobias, and social withdrawal. Summarize our understanding of how they develop and three behavioral principles used in treating them. (p. 425-430)

9. Why has it been difficult to define and measure affective disorders in childhood? Describe the social relationships of these children. (p. 430-431)

EATING DISORDERS (p. 431-435)

10. Define anorexia nervosa and bulimia nervosa noting other
    characteristics associated with them.   Summarize the two steps in
    treating anorexia nervosa. (p. 431-435)

SELF-TEST, CHAPTER 15

MULTIPLE-CHOICE

1. How were early classifications of childhood disorders developed?
   a. extrapolations of adult classifications
   b. based on psychodynamic theory
   c. data from surveys of child clinics
   d. as deviations from developmental norms

2. Keith has been diagnosed as having ADHD. In addition to hyperactive behavior and difficulty paying attention, Keith probably has problems with
   a. academic work.
   b. peer relationships.
   c. impulsivity, leading to poor judgments.
   d. all of the above.

3. The hypothesis that ADHD has a genetic basis
   a. has been proven false; the disorder is more likely caused by environmental stress.
   b. has not been adequately tested.
   c. has been found to be true only for those children whose parents are also antisocial.
   d. has been proven to be true; it is the predisposition for the disorder that is inherited.

4. Which of the following childhood disorders has the worst prognosis?
   a. attention-deficit hyperactivity disorder
   b. conduct disorder - group type
   c. conduct disorder - solitary aggressive type
   d. elective mutism

5. Patterson's coercion hypothesis describes an example of
   a. operant conditioning.
   b. classical conditioning.
   c. punishment.
   d. time out from reinforcement.

6. Brian was enrolled in a program of anger-control training to reduce his aggression. As part of his training, peers were told to insult Brian and he was told to
   a. respond with calm statements to the children, such as "I'm not going to let you upset me."
   b. firmly but politely tell them to stop.
   c. distract himself by humming or turning away.
   d. signal an adult when he was becoming angry.

7. What fear frequently underlies school phobia?
   a. fear of being away from the parent
   b. fear of humiliation by peers
   c. fear of academic demands
   d. fear of the unknown

8. Lefkowitz and Burton (1978) argue that depression should not be diagnosed in children because
   a. their lack of future perspective makes it unlikely that they really feel the hopelessness that defines depression.
   b. this diagnosis would lead to overmedicating children.
   c. the symptoms of adult depression are common and transient in children.
   d. depression is usually masked in childhood.

9. Anorexia nervosa usually begins
   a. around age 10 to 12, just before puberty begins.
   b. in adolescence.
   c. in early adulthood, as the young woman begins to live independently.
   d. during the middle-age crisis.

10. DSM-IIIR catagorizes bulimia nervosa as
   a. a separate eating disorder.
   b. a subtype of anorexia nervosa.
   c. a neurological disorder.
   d. none of the above; obesity is not diagnosed as a mental illness.

SHORT ANSWER

1. Why is it important to remember that problem children are identified by others, not themselves?

2. Why is it difficult to distinguish between ADHD and "just an active kid"?

3. Summarize Feingold's allergy theory of ADHD and research on it's effectiveness.

4. Summarize the research on brain damage as a cause of ADHD.

5. How effective are drug treatments for hyperactivity?

6. Distinguish between two types of conduct disorder.

7. "School phobia" is best understood, not as fear of school, but as fear of . . .

8. Identify several procedures used in helping children overcome childhood fears and social withdrawal.

9. Describe the assumptions behind the "family lunch session" as a treatment for anorexia.

*10. What is known about the causes of anorexia and bulimia?

ANSWERS TO SELF-TEST, CHAPTER 15

MULTIPLE-CHOICE

1. A (p. 412)   2. D (p. 413-416)   3. B (p. 417)   4. C (p. 419)
5. A (p. 423)   6. C (p. 424)   7. A (p. 427)   8. C (p. 430)
9. B (p. 431)   10. A (p. 433)

SHORT ANSWER

1. There's no assurance the child desires help or recognizes having a problem. It may not be the child's problem. (p. 413)

2. The child is referred by others.   The child may not be extremely active - just more active than adults around him or her preferr. (This is also an example of the problem in Question 1 just above) (p. 416)

3. Feingold attributed ADHD to allergies to various food additives. Research indicates his diet helps a small percentage of cases only. (p. 417-418)

4.   Several lines of research indirectly suggest the possibility but no specific kinds of brain damage have been shown to be involved. (p. 418)

5. Drugs reduce behavior problems but they have little effect on (and may harm) academic achievement. (p. 418-419)

6. In "-group type" the individual misbehaves with peers while, in "-solitary aggressive type" the individual misbehaves alone. (p. 419)

7. Separation from home and parents. (p. 427)

8. Expose child to feared situation while providing encouragement and reinforcement.   Provide models and teach skills for appropriate behavior. (p. 427-429)

9. Assumes that not eating deflects attention away from family conflicts thus keeping the family together. (p. 433)

10. Very little.   Many speculations have been offered but none are supported. (p. 432, 435)

16. Learning Disabilities, Mental Retardation, and Autistic Disorder

OVERVIEW

Chapter 16 is the second of three chapters devoted to developmental disorders. The previous chapter covered emotional and behavioral problems. Chapter 16 will cover cognitive, intellectual and skill problems. These are learning disabilities, mental retardation and autistic disorder.

The next chapter (Chapter 17) will deal with problems of aging. Older individual are subject to a wide variety of problems. They must cope with the physical problems of aging. More importantly they must cope with the realization that they are getting older as well as the fact that society often does not seem to respect, value, or provide for them.

After Chapter 17, the next (and last) section of the text focuses on intervention methods and issues.

CHAPTER SUMMARY

Chapter 16 covers three problems. *Learning Disabilities* are developmental delays in specific areas (reading, etc.) not related to general intellectual retardation. Treatment consists of trying to teach the missing specific skills.

A diagnosis of *Mental Retardation* involves three criteria; subnormal intellectual functioning, deficits in adaptive behavior, and onset before age 18. Severe retardation usually results from physical factors including chromosomal abnormalities, diseases, malnutrition, or brain injuries. Mild retardation is much more common and is the center of much social and scientific interest. Social and environmental factors are considered the primary causes. Special educational and social enrichment programs seek to prevent or minimize retardation, particularly under provisions of Public Law 94-142. Educational and behavioral programs are used to treat problems of retarded individuals as well as improve their intellectual functioning.

Autistic Disorder is, fortunately, an uncommon disorder in which very young children show profound problems in speech, learning, and social relations. Research has not supported early theories which suggested that autistic children had been rejected by emotionally cold parents. Physiological causes have been suggested. Treatment of autism is difficult. Behavioral procedures using modeling and operant conditioning seem to reduce some symptoms. However most autistic children remain intellectually and socially limited.

ESSENTIAL CONCEPTS

1. Learning disabilities are specific developmental problems in an isolated area of academic functioning.

2. The diagnostic criteria for mental retardation: are (a) significantly subaverage intellectual functioning; (b) deficits in adaptive behavior; and (c) onset during the developmental period.

3. There are four classification levels of mental retardation (mild, moderate, severe, and profound), with different IQ cutoff scores and prognoses for each level.

4. The specific etiology for most cases of mental retardation is unknown (cultural-familial deprivation and undetected brain impairments are suggested). These cases generally fall in the mild category.

5. Known physical causes of mental retardation include Down's Syndrome, PKU, infectious causes, and fetal alcohol syndrome.

6. Early interventions such as Project Head Start can lead to improvements in intellectual functioning but, once the intervention is withdrawn, regression is common.

7. The deinstitutionalization movement and Public Law 94-142 have radically changed the way the retarded are treated in our society.

8. Infantile autism is characterized by extreme autistic aloneness, severely limited language, and ritualistic behavior.

9. The specific etiology of infantile autism remains unknown, although recent work suggests physiological, rather that psychological, factors.

10. Highly structured social-learning treatments have been successful in reducing self-injury and in improving communication and self-care skills among autistic children.

KEY TERMS

Specific developmental disorders
    (or learning disabilities) (p. 440)

Developmental reading disorder (Dyslexia) (p. 440)

Developmental arithmetic disorder (p. 440)

Developmental expressive writing disorder (p. 440)

Developmental articulation disorder (p. 441)

Developmental coordination disorder (p. 441)

Mental retardation (p. 442)

Down's syndrome (trisomy 21) (p. 450)

Fragile X syndrome (p. 451)

Phenylketonuria (p. 454)

Fetal alcohol syndrome (p. 455)

Deinstitutionalization (p. 457)

Public Law 94-142 (p. 459)

Autistic disorder (p. 463)

Echolalia (p. 465)

Pronoun reversal (p. 466)

Time-out procedure (p. 470)

STUDY QUESTIONS

LEARNING DISABILITIES (p. 440-442)

1. Define specific developmental disorders (or learning disabilities) and give several examples. (p. 440-441)

2. Briefly describe three approaches to the causes of learning disabilities. Describe two common approaches to intervention. (p. 441-442)

MENTAL RETARDATION (p. 442-463)

3. Define "mental retardation" using DSM-IIIR's three criteria. Describe how psychologists decide if someone meets the first two criteria. (p. 442-444)

4. DSM-IIIR classifies four levels of retardation. For each, give (1) the IQ range, (2) the expected degree of social adaptation, and (3) common causes of the problem. (p. 444-446)

5. Identify six adaptive skill areas in which retarded individuals typically show deficits. Why is it frequently inappropriate to describe degree of retardation using age levels. (p. 446-448)

6. Identify two reasons retarded individuals may have deficiencies in their underlying cognitive abilities. Briefly describe research into five cognitive abilities. (p. 448-449)

7. Briefly describe two theories about the cause of retardation with no identifiable organic etiology. Briefly describe seven organic causes of retardation with an example of each. (p. 449-456)

8. Describe two approaches to prevention of mental retardation. How successful has each been? (p. 456-457)

9. Describe two specific efforts to treat retardation. Describe the general current approach by explaining five provisions of Public Law 94-142 and four strategies for teaching retardates. (p. 457-463)

AUTISTIC DISORDER (p. 463-472)

10. Describe autistic disorder in general and it's relation to retardation. Describe three characteristic deficits in autism and the prognosis for autistic children. (p. 463-468)

11. Summarize early psychological theories of autism including the ideas of hopelessness, shutting out the world, and parental roles. How well has research supported these theories?   Describe two research areas suggesting a physiological basis for infantile autism. (p. 468-470)

12. List five reasons why autistic children are especially difficult to treat?   (p. 470)

13. Summarize three illustrations of social-learning approaches to treatment of autistics.   Evaluate two other approaches.   (p. 470-472)

SELF-TEST, CHAPTER 16

MULTIPLE-CHOICE

1. Learning disabilities are called _____ in DSM-IIIR.
   a. dyslexia
   b. academic skills disorders
   c. mental retardation
   d. specific developmental disorders

2. Which would be emphasized in treating specific learning disabilities?
   a. high-protein, low-salt diet
   b. academic preparation
   c. drug treatment of neurological deficits
   d. improved social skills

*3. Most mentally retarded children are identified as such
   a. before birth, through amniocentesis.
   b. during infancy.
   c. when they start school.
   d. when they begin puberty.

*4. What DSM-IIIR label is appropriate for an 9-year-old boy who obtains an IQ of 60 but is doing all right socially and academically?
   a. mild retardation
   b. moderate retardation
   c. cultural-familial retardation
   d. none of the above

5. The term _____ refers to the ability of retarded individuals to solve problems in effective, organized ways.
   a. attention to stimuli
   b. control processes
   c. processing speed
   d. executive functioning

6. Down's syndrome is the result of
   a. environmental insult, usually during the birth process.
   b. a specific chromosomal abnormality.
   c. fragile X.
   d. a recessive-gene disease.

7. In what way has Head Start helped prevent mental retardation?
   a. Graduates functioned better, although deficits remained.
   b. Graduates were less likely to have retarded infants.
   c. Some methods have been successfully used in public schools.
   d. Methods were developed to select those children most likely to
      benefit from intervention.

8. For mentally retarded individuals who have difficulty speaking, the
   most effective means of teaching them to communicate involves
   a. teaching sign language.
   b. behavior modification.
   c. cognitive-behavior therapy.
   d. computer-assisted instruction.

9. Extreme autistic aloneness describes
   a. the autistic child's total detachment from interpersonal
      relationships.
   b. the parents' rejection of the autistic child, leading to extreme
      isolation.
   c. the autistic child's total lack of involvement with people, animals,
      and objects.
   d. the autistic child's sensory deprivation.

10. Which was a core feature of Lovaas' long-term program for very
    young autistics?
    a. elimination of negative reinforcement procedures
    b. a highly controlled environment with little human contact
    c. using normal children as peer therapists
    d. treatment continued almost all the time

SHORT ANSWER

1. Define "specific developmental disorders".

2. Summarize evidence regarding minimal brain damage as a cause of
   learning disabilities.

3. Identify the two major views on psychological factors in learning disabilities.

4. List the three criteria for diagnosing mental retardation in DSM-IIIR.

5. What is "Adaptive behavior" as used in defining mental retardation?

6. Briefly summarize the level of social and academic abilities expected of mildly retarded individuals.

7. Why is it often inappropriate to describe a retarded individual's deficiencies by age level (for example, saying the person "is functioning at the six-year level")?

8. Give examples of many different organic causes of retardation (the text gave six categories).

9. Applied behavior analysis has developed methods of teaching highly retarded individuals to . . .

10. Summarize research on the drug fenfluramine as a treatment for autism.

ANSWERS TO SELF-TEST, CHAPTER 16

MULTIPLE-CHOICE

1. D (p. 440)   2. B (p. 441-442)   3. C (p. 444)   4. D (p. 442-444)
5. D (p. 449)   6. B (p. 450-451)   7. A (p. 457)   8. A (p. 462)
9. A (p. 464-465) 10. D (p. 471)

SHORT ANSWER

1. Learning disabilities: deficits in development of specific intellectual skills such as reading, arithmetic, language and speech. (p. 440)

2. Studies do not confirm this view. (p. 441)

3. Deficits in perception of stimuli, poor teaching, education. (p. 441)

4. A) Significantly subaverage intelligence, B) Deficits in adaptive behavior, C) Manifest during the developmental period. (p. 443-444)

5. Adaptive behavior meets standards of personal independence & social responsibility appropriate to individual's age & culture. (p. 443-444)

6. As children they are not obviously different until they enter school. Academic skills usually limited to about sixth grade. As adults perform unskilled jobs and live in society but may need guidance with finances etc. (p. 445)

7. Because different skills may not develop equally. Especially social skills and interests of a retarded adult aren't often comparable to those of a child. (p. 447-448)

8. 1) Genetic conditions such as Down's syndrome, PKU, 2) Infectious diseases effecting pregnant mother (rubella, syphilis, etc) or child (meningitis, etc), 3) accident, injury, 4) Premature birth (possibly), 5) Chemical substances (thalidomide, alcohol, etc.), 6) Environmental hazards including pollutants in air, food, paint, etc. (p. 450-456)

9. Feed, groom, & care for themselves. Not injure selves. (p. 460-461)

10. Autistics received fenfluramine or a placebo in alternation. Parents and observers, who did not know which drug was being given, rated improvement in IQ and behavior for some autistics. (p. 472)

17. Aging and Psychological Disorders

OVERVIEW

Chapter 17 is the last of three chapters on developmental disorders. The first two chapters discussed disorders of childhood and growing up. Chapter 15 covered emotional and behavioral problems while Chapter 16 dealt with cognitive and skill problems. Chapter 17 is devoted to the problems of aging and growing old.

Chapter 17 completes the text's discussion of psychological disorders. The next, and last, section of the text deals more intensively with topics covered only briefly so far. Three chapters will intensively discuss treatment methods. The last chapter will cover legal and ethical issues.

CHAPTER SUMMARY

Growing old is, obviously, a time of physical decline and medical problems become an increasing concern. Beyond the purely medical aspects of old age, however, are a wide range of psychological and social problems.

The chapter begins by summarizing *Concepts and Methods in the Study of Older Adults*. It then gives *Some Basic Facts About Older Adults* including some realistic problems facing the elderly. This discussion forms a basis for considering the physical and psychological disorders of the elderly.

Brain Disorders of Old Age may be slowly developing, progressive, dementias that are usually irreversible and require supportive care. They may also be sudden deliriums that can often be reversed by treating the underlying physical conditions.

The difficulties of growing old also make the elderly especially subject to various *Psychological Problems of Old Age*. Depression often accompanies physical and psychological declines as people grow old. Suspiciousness and paranoia may result as the elderly experience difficulty understanding others due to hearing problems and social isolation. The elderly are also subject to other psychological problems. Suicide may result as the elderly struggle to accept changing physical and social situations. Contrary to popular conceptions, the elderly are capable of enjoying and engaging in sexual activity despite slowed physiological responses.

The chapter concludes with a discussion of *General Issues in Treatment and Care* of the elderly. Nursing homes and other facilities often fail to encourage the elderly to maintain their skills and capabilities. Community-based services could help the elderly remain as independent as possible. Psychotherapy can also help the elderly accept changes and provide them support and information to continue functioning.

ESSENTIAL CONCEPTS

1. Age effects, cohort effects, and time-of-measurement effects complicate research efforts to understand the elderly.

2. The proportion of aged individuals in the population of the United States has been and will continue to grow.

3. When interpreting data representing the aged, it is important to remember that the prevalence of chronic physical illnesses is great among the aged, poverty rates are higher than for younger age groups, housing is less adequate, prejudice exists, and many major life events (e.g. death of loved ones) have been experienced.

4. Dementia is a gradual deterioration of intellectual abilities over several years until functioning becomes impaired.

5. Many cases of dementia are irreversible. Treatment consists of support and assistance in living as independently as possible.

6. Most dementia patients are in the care of their families and support for these families is valuable, specially when they must decide about institutionalization.

7. Delirium is a clouded state of consciousness characterized by difficulty in concentrating and maintaining a directed stream of though. Many cases of delirium are reversible if detected in time.

8. There is a tendency to attribute the behavior of the aged to the fact that they are older. This can lead to erroneous conclusions about the effects of aging and cause us to overlook the individual's uniqueness.

9. Despite assumptions to the contrary, psychological problems such as depression, paranoid disorder, substance abuse, and hypochondria may actually be less prevalent among the aged than among younger groups.

10. Most older adults maintain sexual interest and engage in sexual activity although there may be a general slowing of the sexual response cycle and the intensity of sexual arousal may not be as great.

11. Regardless of whether they are cared for in the community or in a nursing home, giving the aged responsibility for self-care, planning, and control over their lives is important to their continued psychological and physical well-being.

KEY TERMS

Age effects (p. 477)

Cohort effects (p. 477)

Time of measurement effects (p. 477-478)

Cross-sectional and longitudinal research (p. 477-478)

Fluid and crystallized intelligence (p. 481)

Dementia (p. 485)

Delirium (p. 489)

Delusional (Paranoid) Disorders (p. 494)

STUDY QUESTIONS

CONCEPTS & METHODS IN THE STUDY OF OLDER ADULTS (p. 476-478)

1. Identify four basic concepts in studying older adults (including three measurement effects that make data difficult to interpret). (p. 476-478

SOME BASIC FACTS ABOUT OLDER ADULTS (p. 478-485)

2. Summarize ten basic facts about older adults (p. 478-485)

BRAIN DISORDERS OF OLD AGE (p. 485-491)

3. Describe two forms of brain disorder that often affect the elderly. Distinguish between symptoms of the two disorders. Describe treatment for each disorder including issues facing families of the victim. (p. 485-491)

PSYCHOLOGICAL DISORDERS OF OLD AGE (p. 491-504)

4. Why has little attention been paid to psychological problems in the elderly? (p. 491) Identify eight psychological problems covered in this section. (p. 491-504)

5. The text describes depression and delusional disorders (paranoia) in depth. For each problem describe; how it differs in older people, possible causes, and treatment. (p. 491-495)

6. Briefly describe two or three issues for each of the following topics; A) schizophrenia, B) alcohol/drug abuse and, C) medication misuse in the elderly. (p. 496-499)

7. Describe the causes and treatment of three other psychological problems among the elderly. (p. 499-501)

8. How does sexual activity change with age? Briefly describe the social and physiological bases for these changes. (p. 501-504)

GENERAL ISSUES IN TREATMENT AND CARE (p. 504-509)

9. Identify two reasons the elderly do not receive their just share of mental health services. (p. 504-505)

10. What kinds of overt problems have been found in nursing homes. Summarize a study suggesting there are also more subtle, basic problems in nursing home care.   What kinds of community-based care could be helpful to the elderly? (p. 505-508)

11. Summarize the major content and process issues in providing therapy to older adults. (p. 509)

SELF-TEST, CHAPTER 17

MULTIPLE-CHOICE

1. A problem with interpreting results from longitudinal studies of aging is
   a. cohort effects are not controlled for.
   b. the changes found may be the result of aging effects, not cohort effects.
   c. the findings may not generalize to other cohorts.
   d. the most active and healthy subjects may drop out of the study, leading to pessimistic findings about aging.

2. Which of the following statements about older adults is true?
   a. Men live longer than women on the average.
   b. The number of very old people is expected to increase.
   c. Clear declines in verbal intelligence begin about age 60.
   d. Increasing numbers of elderly live in institutional settings.

3. Impairment in the following area is necessary for a diagnosis of dementia:
   a. abstract thinking
   b. judgment
   c. language
   d. memory

4. Traci complained to the psychologist she was seeing that she was having great difficulty remembering things. On a standardized memory tests, Traci refused to answer many of the questions, saying they were too difficult; on those questions she did answer, however, she performed at an average level. Which of the following diagnoses is more likely?
   a. dementia (early stage)
   b. small stroke
   c. depression
   d. delusional (paranoid) disorder

5. Which of the following is a serious potential consequence of alcoholism in old age?
   a. delirium
   b. cognitive deficits
   c. impaired social relationships
   d. all of the above

6. What is a common cause of hypocondriasis among older individuals?
   a. Their generation expresses concerns in physical terms.
   b. Complaints lead others to pay more attention to them.
   c. Actual physical problems leads to over-reporting symptoms.
   d. They have more free time to ruminate on their troubles.

7. Why do women tend to have less sexual activity in old age than men?
   a. they have more decline in their sexual functioning
   b. they are less likely to have a sexual partner
   c. they have a greater decrease in sexual desire
   d. all of the above

8. Studies on the efficacy of therapy with older adults demonstrate that it is
   a. as effective as with younger adults.
   b. less effective than with younger adults.
   c. as effective as long as insight-oriented approaches are avoided.
   d. as effective as long as behavioral approaches are avoided.

9. Which of the following is a subtle cause of decline in nursing home residents?
   a. unsafe and unsanitary conditions
   b. lack of procedures to reduce the spread of infections
   c. helping residents to do things that they could do themselves
   d. lack of psychotropic medications

10. What is often a useful focus in psychotherapy with older adults?
    a. diverting attention from thoughts of death
    b. examining philosophical and religious values
    c. encouraging patients not to overexert themselves
    d. providing the best possible custodial care

SHORT ANSWER

1. If older people are more socially conservative this may be not because people get more conservative as they get older but because older people grew up in more conservative times. This would be called a _____. effect

2. How serious a problem are physical illnesses for most older people?

3. How significant are learning and memory loses for most older people?

4. How may societal expectations about old age effect older individuals?

5. Define "dementia"

6. List several common causes of delirium in older people.

7. Most psychological disorders in older people result from . . .

8. What appears to be the most effective treatment for insomnia and sleeplessness among the elderly?

9. What happens to sexual interests and activity as people get older?

10. Community-based services for the elderly should attempt to . . .

ANSWERS TO SELF-TEST, CHAPTER 17

MULTIPLE-CHOICE

1. C (p. 477)   2. B (p. 478-484)   3. D (p. 485)   4. C (p. 493)
5. D (p. 498)   6. A (p. 499)   7. B (p. 501-502)   8. A (p. 505)
9. C (p. 505-506)   10. B (p. 509)

SHORT ANSWER

1. age (p. 477)

2. Older people do decline physically and chronic illnesses are common but most are not severely limited by physical illnesses at least until after 75. (p. 479-480)

3. Research shows some slowing but this may be of little practical significance. (p. 481-482)

4. Older people may be treated as more limited than they are thus indirectly encouraging their decline. (p. 484)

5. Gradual deterioration of intellectual abilities to point that social & occupational functioning is impaired. (p. 485)

6. Intoxication from prescription drugs, metabolic & nutritional imbalances, illness, stress. (p. 490)

7. Struggles to cope with realistic problems of getting old plus existing personality problems. (Not old age or physical decline as such typically) (p. 491)

8. Reassurance that they need less sleep. Training in relaxation and good sleep habits. (p. 500-501)

9. They continue to have considerable sexual interest and capacity. Some physical slowing occurs but interest may remain high. (p. 501-502)

10. Provide a range of services which can be matched to individual needs in order to encourage the elderly to live as independently as possible. (p. 507-509)

18. Insight Therapy

OVERVIEW

The previous chapter completed the text's discussion of major forms of abnormal behavior. Chapter 18 begins the last section of the text which describes major forms of treatment and related issues.

The first two chapters in this section discuss types of insight therapy and behavior therapy. These are the two major approaches to treatment in contemporary psychology. Chapter 20 will discuss other major approaches to treating psychological problems. Chapter 21 deals with legal and ethical issues in treatment.

CHAPTER SUMMARY

Insight therapies (Chapter 18) most closely fit the general understanding of "psychotherapy". Research into psychotherapy is complicated by *The Placebo Effect*, the tendency of patients to improve due to general factors rather than specific techniques.

Insight therapies assume that behavior changes as clients develop increased awareness of themselves and the conscious or unconscious motivations behind their behavior. Two major schools have emerged. *Psychoanalytic Therapy*, following Freud, sees problems as arising because individuals have never resolved childhood conflicts between their inner desires and external social reality demands. Psychoanalysis tries to uncover these repressed conflicts so they may be re-examined from an adult perspective.

Humanistic and Existential Therapies focus more on potentials for psychological growth and on factors that may inhibit and distort that growth. Humanists such as Rogers stress nonjudgmental acceptance by the therapist enabling clients to understand themselves more accurately and to trust their inner desires for growth. Existentialists agree that all individuals have an inner drive to grow while emphasizing each person's ability to make choices. Both schools emphasize the need for therapists to understand and accept the client's perspective.

Perls' gestalt therapy is a variation on humanistic therapy which emphasizes living in the present and uses many techniques to help clients become aware of and accept their present feelings.

There is little research to show that improvement during insight therapy occurs for the reasons emphasized by the various theories. Some theorists deny that therapy can be understood and studied using scientific research methods.

ESSENTIAL CONCEPTS

1. Psychotherapy is an interpersonal influence process that is not easily distinguished from other helping relationships (such as friendships). Professionals typically work with people who have not been helped elsewhere.

2. The placebo effect, a part of all therapies, refers to an improvement that is attributable to expectations of help, rather than to a specific active ingredient.

3. Insight is the major goal of psychoanalytic, humanistic, existential, and gestalt therapies.

4. In traditional psychoanalysis, free associations, resistance, dream analysis, interpretation, and transference are major therapeutic tools used to achieve insight.

5. Ego analysts share many of Freud's views but place greater emphasis on the conscious mind and are more likely to deal with current problems by being directive as well as analyzing the past.

6. Research generally does not provide strong support regarding the effectiveness of analytic therapy when compared to improvement over time, although the concepts in analytic therapy make it particularly difficult to evaluate.

7. Psychotherapy outcome research evaluates the effectiveness of a treatment in comparison to an alternative such as no treatment while psychotherapy process research links therapeutic interactions with therapy outcome.

8. The concept of free will is emphasized by humanistic, existential, and Gestalt therapists.

9. Carl Rogers argued that therapy should be directed by the client, and that the therapist's major goal is to help the client by being warm, genuine, and empathetic.

10. Existential therapists emphasize authenticity, awareness, and the exercise of free choice - which carries with it the confrontation of painful human realities. Thus they are less optimistic than humanistic therapists.

11. Fritz Perls' Gestalt therapy highlights the here and now and makes use of a variety of techniques in order to help people become aware of their present desires.

KEY TERMS

Insight (vs. action) therapy (p. 515)

Placebo effect (p. 515)

Psychoanalysis (p. 516)

Free association (p. 516)

Resistance (p. 517)

Manifest & latent content (p. 517)

Transference neurosis (p. 518)

Countertransference (p. 518)

Ego analysis (p. 519-520)

Outcome and process studies (p. 521)

Brief therapy (p. 523)

Client-centered therapy (p. 524)

Unconditional positive regard (p. 525)

Empathy (p. 525)

Existential therapy (p. 528)

Gestalt therapy (p. 530)

STUDY QUESTIONS

1. What is "psychotherapy" and why is it difficult to define? (p. 514-515)

THE PLACEBO EFFECT (p. 515-516)

2. What is the placebo effect?   How is it better understood in
   psychotherapy?   (p. 515-516)

PSYCHOANALYTIC THERAPY (p. 516-524)

3. What is the basic assumption of psychoanalysis?   Describe seven
   techniques of psychoanalysis and how each contributes to treatment.
   (p. 516-519)

4. How do ego analysts differ from classical analysts in their views on
   (1) the role of the ego and (2) the source of energy or gratification
   for the ego? (p. 519-521)

224

5. Give two reasons why has it been difficult to evaluate therapy ? Briefly summarize outcome research on classical psychoanalysis. (p. 521-522)

6. Use the Temple University Outpatient research to illustrate outcome research problems of 1) measuring outcome, 2) comparing therapies and 3) comparing what therapists actually do. What is the problem of process research? (p. 522-524)

HUMANISTIC & EXISTENTIAL THERAPIES (p. 524-534)

7. Explain five assumptions of Carl Roger's Client-centered therapy. (p. 524-525)

8. What is the role of a Rogerian therapist?   Describe three qualities of
   a therapist in this role explaining the importance of the third quality.
   (p. 525-527)

9. What kind of research has Rogers done to evaluate his theory and
   with what results?   Identify five criticisms of his theory. (p. 527-
   528)

10. According to existential philosophy, what is the relationship
   between self-awareness, making choices, being responsible, and
   existential anxiety.   (p. 528-529)

11. Summarize four goals of existential therapy. Why do existentialists reject scientific evaluation of their approach? (p. 529-530)

12. Summarize the basic concepts of Perls' Gestalt therapy in terms of (1) the influence of individual needs, (2) the individual as actor, and (3) the here and now. Give some examples of Gestalt techniques. (p. 530-533)

13. Summarize the text's evaluation of Gestalt therapy in six points. (Look for: overall evaluation, theoretical parsimony, strengths and weaknesses of Gestalt "responsibility", view of human goodness, Perls as an individual, and potential for abuse.) (p. 533-534)

SELF-TEST, CHAPTER 18

MULTIPLE-CHOICE

1. Why are placebo control groups used in therapy outcome studies?
   a. to determine whether the theory of psychotherapy being tested is responsible for the improvement found
   b. to determine whether the patients would improve without any treatment
   c. to determine which therapists produce the most improvement
   d. to determine how susceptible patients are to suggestion

2. Which of the following is an example of the psychoanalytic concept of resistance?
   a. asking the analyst how many children she has
   b. reporting trivial episodes from childhood that are unrelated to the topic being discussed
   c. crying
   d. interrupting the analyst

3. How do ego analysts view the ego differently than classical Freudian analysts?
   a. as largely unconscious
   b. as having it's own drives and energies
   c. as present in all people
   d. as developing from the id

4. The following criticism has been made of the Temple University Outpatient Clinic study (Sloane et al., 1975):
   a. lack of multiple sources of information on patient functioning
   b. lack of a control group
   c. lack of experienced therapists
   d. lack of observational measures of patient functioning

5. According to Carl Rogers, the paths people take in life are due primarily to
   a. the influence of their childhood experiences.
   b. their own self-direction.
   c. the press of instinctual impulses.
   d. the impact of their present environment.

*6. In the first session of client-centered therapy, which type of
    empathy would probably be used most?
    a. advanced accurate empathy
    b. primary empathy
    c. interpretive empathy
    d. phenomenological empathy

7. Traditionally, client-centered therapy researchers have used the
   following as outcome measure(s):
   a. client's self-report
   b. observations of behavior
   c. therapist's assessment of change in symptoms
   d. all of the above

8. In existential therapy the concept of "Becoming" means that
   a. present problems reflect past conflicts
   b. behavior change follows insight and increased awareness
   c. people are constantly evolving
   d. people have the capacity for self-awareness

9. Which therapy focuses on helping people become more aware of their
   here-and-now experiences and desires?
   a. psychoanalysis
   b. client centered
   c. existential
   d. Gestalt

10. In Gestalt therapy, responsibility for the client's behavior and
    feelings is placed on
    a. the client.
    b. the therapist.
    c. the client's parents.
    d. current influences in the environment.

SHORT ANSWER

1. What is the basic assumption of insight psychotherapy?

2. Why do psychoanalysts attempt to remain detached from their
   patients?

3. Briefly describe how ego analysts view people (as compared to traditional psychoanalysis).

4. What kinds of people and problems are most likely to benefit from psychoanalysis?

5. Summarize current views on the effectiveness of psychoanalysis.

6. Summarize Carl Roger's view of personality development and growth.

7. The text criticizes Rogerian-based therapy research for not paying enough attention to . . .

8. Why do existential therapists avoid doing research on the effectiveness of their techniques?

9. What is the general purpose of gestalt therapy techniques?

10. What do Gestalt therapists such as Perls urge clients to be responsible for?

ANSWERS TO SELF-TEST, CHAPTER 18

MULTIPLE-CHOICE

1. A (p. 515-516) 2. A (p. 517)   3. B (p 520-521) 4. D (p. 522-523)
5. B (p. 524-525) 6. B (p. 526-527) 7. A (p. 527)   8. C (p. 528-529)
9. D (p. 531)   10. A (p. 531)

SHORT ANSWER

1. That people can control and change behavior if they develop understanding of what causes or motivates it. (p. 515)

2. They feel that offering suggestions and comfort would provide short-term help at best and would delay development of transference and long-term improvement. (p. 516)

3. View people as able to control their environment and instinctual drives enabling them to postpone and control urges. (p. 520-521)

4. Educated verbal people with anxiety problems (not psychotic) (p. 522)

5. It's effectiveness is difficult to measure. It is not clearly more effective than other methods, placebos, or simply passage of time. (p. 522)

6. People innately seek to grow, to actualize or develop their potentials, and will seek ways to do so. (p. 524-525)

7. How people's actual behavior changes following therapy. (p. 527)

8. Their therapy is based on philosophical, not scientific, views. They consider science dehumanizing. (p. 530)

9. Help clients get in touch with here-and-now feelings. (p. 531-532)

10. Taking care of themselves by recognizing and accepting responsibility for meeting their own needs. (p. 532)

19. Cognitive and Behavior Therapies

OVERVIEW

Chapter 19 is the second of three chapters on therapies for psychological problems. Chapters 18 and 19 discuss the two major approaches to therapy in contemporary psychology: insight and behavior therapies. Insight approaches grew primarily out of the experiences of therapists talking with disturbed individuals. In contrast, behavior therapies grew out of scientific research traditions within psychology. Insight therapies seek to develop increased self-insight and awareness on the assumption that behavior will change naturally as individuals understand the bases for their disordered actions. Behavior therapies use scientific principles to study disordered behavior and to develop methods for changing it.

After Chapter 19 the text will discuss some other popular therapy techniques such as group, family, community, and somatic therapy. The last chapter will cover legal and ethical issues in abnormal psychology.

CHAPTER SUMMARY

Chapter 19 summarizes a variety of behavior therapies which have developed out of research models of behavior. *Counterconditioning* seeks to change classically conditioned responses to stimuli. For example, systematic desensitization seeks to eliminate unrealistic fear responses by gradually introducing the stimulus under anxiety inhibiting conditions.

Operant Conditioning uses rewards & punishment to modify behaviors. For example, token economies systematically reward appropriate behaviors among hospitalized patients. *Modeling* & imitation are used to teach a wide variety of complex responses to situations.

As behavior therapy has matured, behavior therapists have developed procedures less obviously tied to traditional behaviorist principles. *Cognitive Restructuring* procedures identify and change belief systems that may lead to inappropriate behaviors. Other behaviorists have developed *Behavioral Medicine* which applies scientific principles to the psychological aspects of traditionally medical problems.

Behavioral therapists have been especially interested in methods to insure *Generalization and Maintenance of Treatment Effects.* Therapists wonder whether the seeming distinctions between traditional insight and behavior therapies are fundamental or superficial. Such *Basic Issues in Behavioral Therapy* remain although, with the newer behavioral approaches, many are becoming increasingly blurred.

ESSENTIAL CONCEPTS

1. Behavior therapy involves the application of procedures developed by experimental psychologists. It is characterized more by its search for rigorous standards of proof than by allegiance to a particular set of concepts.

2. In counterconditioning a response to a given stimulus is eliminated by eliciting different behavior in the presence of the stimulus.

3. Systematic desensitization is a counterconditioning fear reduction technique that involves pairing, through imagination, increasingly feared events with a simultaneous state of deep relaxation.

4. Aversion therapy involves pairing an aversive stimulus with an unwanted thought, emotion, or behavior in order to reduce it. There are questions about the ethics and efficacy of aversion therapy.

5. Operant conditioning therapy techniques involve the delineation of rules of expected behavior and the systematic reinforcement of behavior which meets these rules. They seem to work best with clients having limited cognitive capabilities and in situations where the therapist can exercise considerable environmental control.

6. Modeling techniques have been used to help treat a wide variety of problems. Modeling involves more than simple imitation and would appear to rely upon a complex set of cognitive processes.

7. Behavior therapies increasingly focused on techniques for altering cognitive processes. Rational-emotive therapy, Beck's cognitive therapy, and social problem solving are examples of cognitive restructuring techniques.

8. Cognitive behavior therapists, in some ways, are returning to the early mentalistic roots of experimental psychology while retaining the emphasis on behavior change as a therapeutic goal.

9. The cognitive behavior therapist is interested in the way the client perceives the world. This is bringing behavior therapy closer to humanistic and existentialist views.

10. Behavioral medicine involves the integration of behavioral and medical science so as to aid in the prevention, diagnosis, treatment and rehabilitation of medical diseases.

11. Any therapy is concerned with the generalization and maintenance of treatment effects to other settings. Behavioral therapists have identified techniques specifically to promote generalization.

12. There are some who see a rapprochement emerging between behavior therapy and psychoanalysis as analysts promote more concrete changes and behaviorists become more sensitive to subtle factors.

KEY TERMS

Behavior therapy (p. 538)

Counter-conditioning (p. 538)

Systematic desensitization (p. 538-539)

Aversion therapy (p. 541)

Token economy (p. 542)

Modeling (p. 546)

Cognitive restructuring (p. 547)

Rational-emotional therapy (p. 547)

Systematic rational restructuring (p. 548-549)

Social problem solving (p. 553)

Triadic reciprocality (p. 558)

Behavioral medicine (p. 558)

Biofeedback (p. 562)

STUDY QUESTIONS

1. What is "behavior therapy"? What does it assume? (p. 538)

COUNTERCONDITIONING (p. 538-542)

2. What is the basic principle of counterconditioning? Describe two counterconditioning methods and their effectiveness. What additional question has been raised about each. (p. 538-542)

OPERANT CONDITIONING (p. 542-546)

3. What is the basic idea of operant conditioning therapies. As an example of operant therapy, describe token economies. How well have they worked (and why aren't they used more)? How are operant principles applied to children? (p. 542-546)

MODELING (p. 546-547)

4. Briefly describe several uses of modeling techniques. How did modeling approaches generate interest in the role of cognition? (p. 546-547)

COGNITIVE RESTRUCTURING (p. 547-558)

5. What is cognitive restructuring and how has Ellis applied it? With what situations does Ellis' approach show promise - and what ethical or philosophical dilemma does it raise? (p. 547-550)

6. Describe Beck's cognitive approach and it's effectiveness. How does Beck's approach compare to Ellis' approach? (p. 550-552)

7. Describe the cognitive therapy of social problem solving. Summarize four reflections or comments on cognitive behavior therapy in general. (p. 552-558)

BEHAVIORAL MEDICINE (p. 558-563)

8. How is behavioral medicine best defined?   Describe   behavioral
   medicine applications in three areas. (p. 558-563)

GENERALIZATION AND MAINTENANCE OF TREATMENT EFFECTS (p. 563-566)

9. What forms of therapy need to be concerned about generalization of
   treatment results?   Describe six methods used by behavior therapists
   to increase generalization. (p. 563-566)

SOME BASIC ISSUES IN BEHAVIOR THERAPY (p. 566-571)

10. Summarize six basic issues underlying contemporary behavior
    therapy. (p. 566-568)

11. What synthesis of psychoanalysis and behavior therapy does Wachtel suggest?   Identify five possible benefits of this rapprochement. - and an underlying issue brought out by a critique of Wachtel. (p. 569-571)

SELF-TEST, CHAPTER 19

MULTIPLE-CHOICE

1. The first step in a systematic desensitization session is
    a. going to the site of the anxiety in person.
    b. imagining a frightening situation.
    c. getting into a deeply relaxed state.
    d. recounting the first experience in which the phobia started.

2. Which of the following problems might be treated using aversion therapy?
    a. fear of public-speaking
    b. avoidant personality disorder
    c. exhibitionism
    d. premature ejaculation

3. Research on operant conditioning with retarded children has found that
    a. such children are not usually trainable.
    b. operant conditioning is inferior to classical conditioning with these children.
    c. such children find few things rewarding, making it difficult (but not impossible) to come up with reinforcers.
    d. it is a highly effective means of teaching many skills.

4. Modeling procedures were important because they showed behavior therapists the importance of
    a. sticking to observable behaviors
    b. classical conditioning
    c. operant conditioning
    d. cognitive processes

5. What ethical issue has been raised regarding Ellis' rational-emotive therapy?
    a. Is it irrational to want to improve oneself?
    b. Should therapists try to change deeply felt beliefs?
    c. Are some beliefs really more rational than others?
    d. Are irrational beliefs necessarily wrong?

6. Client: "I am depressed all the time, from morning to night, day in and day out. I just can't shake it, no matter what I do." Which of the following responses would be most characteristic of Aaron Beck's approach to therapy?
   a. "It must be very painful to feel unhappy all of the time."
   b. "What do you have to be depressed about?"
   c. "I'd like you to monitor your mood every few hours for the next week, so we can get a clearer idea of what your moods are like."
   d. "Your depression is based on irrational statements you are making to yourself; let's find out what some of those self-statements might be."

7. In contrast to the traditional behavioral view of distress, cognitive-behavior therapists now emphasize
   a. the influence that the environment has on our thoughts and feelings.
   b. the importance of childhood experiences.
   c. the impact of our world view on our feelings and behavior.
   d. free will and self-determinism.

8. What does the field of behavioral medicine provide?
   a. medical procedures to help psychological problems
   b. psychological procedures to help physical conditions
   c. psychological alternatives to medical treatment
   d. medical practitioners in psychological treatment settings

9. What procedure is this? Joe's therapist emphasizes that improvements are due to Joe's work and effort rather than the therapist's skill.
   a. attribution to self
   b. self-reinforcement
   c. relapse prevention
   d. eliminating secondary gain

10. Attention-placebo control groups in psychotherapy outcome studies have demonstrated the importance of
    a. the client-therapist relationship.
    b. empathy.
    c. secondary gain.
    d. the unconscious.

SHORT ANSWER

1. Describe the method of aversion therapy.

2. Briefly summarize two reasons that aversion therapy is controversial.

3. Why aren't token economies used more?

4. Explain how modeling is used in behavioral therapy.

5. How does Ellis go about helping people change their irrational self-statements in rational-emotive therapy?

6. How does Beck's therapeutic approach differ from that of Ellis?

7. In what way is behavioral therapy becoming similar to humanistic & existential therapy?

8. What is "behavioral medicine".

9. Briefly describe six methods used to promote generalization of treatment changes.

10. Do behavioral therapists deal with symptoms or with the true causes of behavior? Explain.

ANSWERS TO SELF-TEST, CHAPTER 19

MULTIPLE-CHOICE

1. C (p. 538)   2. C (p. 541)   3. D (p. 545-546)   4. D (p. 547)
5. D (p. 549)   6. C (p. 550-551) 7. C (p. 558)   8. B (p. 558-559)
9. A (p. 566)   10. A (p. 568)

SHORT ANSWER

1. Negative feelings are attached to inappropriately attractive stimuli by pairing the stimuli with unpleasant events. (p. 541)

2. A) Ethics of inflicting pain even when clients agree, B) Effectiveness doubtful unless combined with other methods. (p. 541)

3. Hospital staff resist them. Token economies require extra effort, expense, contradict traditional views, raise questions, etc. (p. 545)

4. Someone models or demonstrates desirable or effective behavior for client to imitate. (p. 546)

5. By using rational explanation and persuasive logic. Helps client realize their self-talk is irrational & leads to problems. (p. 547-549)

6. Beck collaborates with client as they seek to discover ineffective assumptions together. Ellis identifies irrationality & explains it to client. (p. 552)

7. Behavior therapy is coming to emphasize cognitive methods which share, with humanism, the view that our perceptions and understandings of the world are the cause of behavior. (p. 558)

8. Combines behavioral & medical fields to develop psychological procedures for improving physical health and treating physical problems. (p. 558-559)

9. Use of intermittent reinforcement, Modify environment to support changed behavior, Encourage clients to recognize and reinforce themselves for good behavior, Eliminating "secondary gain", Help clients cope with and not become discouraged by relapses, Encourage clients to attribute results to their own efforts. (p. 506-507

10. Behaviorists do not assume true causes must involve unconscious or childhood factors. They seek the most important causes of behavior which may be in the current situation. (p. 567)

20. Group, Family, and Marital Therapy, and Community Psychology

OVERVIEW

This is the last of three chapters exploring various treatment approaches. The previous two chapters presented insight and behavior therapies as two primary approaches to treatment. Despite marked differences in both goals and methods, these two approaches were seen as moving to a rapprochement at the end of Chapter 19. Chapter 20 discusses three other approaches to treatment: group therapy, couples & family therapy and community psychology.

The final chapter of the text will cover legal and ethical issues in abnormal psychology. Psychologists are often faced with dilemmas as they try to protect the rights of both their clients and of larger society. Legal issues will include criminal commitment (legal insanity, and competency to stand trial) and civil commitment for individuals judged dangerous to themselves or others. Ethical issues involve efforts to define and protect the rights of individuals as both therapy clients and research participants.

CHAPTER SUMMARY

Chapter 20 discusses three other approaches to treatment, each with it's own unique strengths. *Group Therapy* is most obviously related to the insight and behavior therapies. Insight-oriented therapy groups offer opportunities to share with and learn from others and to get behind social facades. Behavior therapy is often done in groups, primarily for economic reasons. *Couple and Family therapy* views conflict as normal in any long-term family system and seeks to help the system cope with problems it's members are experiencing.

Community Psychology seeks to prevent problems from developing by promoting changes in groups, communities, and society at large. Often community psychology is carried out in community mental health centers which work within the community to prevent or alleviate problems. Prevention of problems has remained, however, an elusive goal.

ESSENTIAL CONCEPTS

1. Although economic efficiency is one rational for group therapy, most therapists suggest that there are additional unique benefits to group therapy, such as vicarious learning, group pressure to change, and the support in knowing that a problem is experienced by others.

2. T-groups and sensitivity training groups are commonly used as growth experiences for well-functioning individuals. Learning to become more honest and open with others and obtaining feedback on interpersonal relationships are among the primary goals of these groups.

3. Many behavior therapy groups are used to provide treatment more economically. Other behavior therapy groups use the group to train skills that only can be learned in a group setting.

4. Research on group therapy, especially process research, is exceedingly difficult to conduct.

5. Couple and marital therapists attribute many psychological difficulties to problems in family relationships. Therapists with this orientation see family members conjointly and emphasize the importance of dealing with interpersonal conflicts and improving communication.

6. Community psychologists focus on the prevention of emotional disturbance using primary, secondary, and tertiary prevention.

7. Given their focus on prevention, community psychologists are likely to operate in the seeking mode rather than the waiting mode and are likely to target their interventions at the organizational or institutional levels rather than at the individual or small group levels.

8. Community mental health centers, suicide prevention centers, the use of the media to try to change life styles, halfway houses, and environmental psychology are all examples of community psychology efforts.

KEY TERMS

Sensitivity training (p. 574)

Encounter groups (p. 574)

Conjoint therapy (p. 581)

Prevention (primary, secondary, tertiary) (p. 586)

Waiting mode & seeking mode (p. 587)

STUDY QUESTIONS

GROUP THERAPY (p. 574-580)

1. Identify three ways group therapy can be useful for accomplishing certain goals. (p. 574)

2. What are the goals of sensitivity training or encounter groups ()also called T-groups)?   How does looking at levels of communication facilitate these goals? (p. 574-576)

3. What are the goals of most behavior therapy groups?   Give several examples of these groups. (p. 576-578)

4. Evaluate group therapy in terms of testimonials, transfer of skills, and adequacy of research. In general, according to research, what are the benefits of group therapy (especially in self-concept and social functioning)? (p. 578-579)

COUPLES AND FAMILY THERAPY (p. 580-586)

5. Why is conflict normal in a long-term relationship? Give some
   examples of how individual therapy approaches are applied to
   families. (p. 580-583)

6. Describe four ways conjoint therapists focus on faulty
   communication (caring days, pleasing each other, intent vs impact,
   and videotaped sessions.) (p. 583-585)

7. How might marital therapy concepts be applied to nonmarital
   problems and divorce? Summarize research into marital and family
   therapy. (p. 585-586)

COMMUNITY PSYCHOLOGY (p. 586-597)

8. Summarize the community psychology approach using the topics of: prevention, delivery mode, and the influence of social values. (p. 586-589)

9. Describe community mental health centers in terms of their objectives, use of paraprofessionals, and emphasis on education. Describe and evaluate five examples of community-oriented mental health programs. (p. 589-595)

10. Evaluate the effectiveness of community psychology in three areas. What social and ethical issues continue in community psychology? (p. 595-597)

SELF-TEST, CHAPTER 20

MULTIPLE-CHOICE

1. Which is a particular benefit of group therapy?
   a. opportunity for lonely people to meet others
   b. support from discovering others have similar problems
   c. more rapid treatment of socially based problems
   d. reduction of social prejudices

2. The focus of T-groups is usually
   a. gaining insight into the historical causes for one's interpersonal problems.
   b. "here and now" relationships with people.
   c. encouraging the expression of anger.
   d. encouraging feelings of commitment and responsibility in intimate relationships.

3. Which group would be particularly useful for a college male who is unable to ask girls for dates?
   a. sensitivity training group
   b. assertion training group
   c. conjoint group
   d. T-group

4. A particular problem of T-groups is
   a. secondary gain
   b. transfer of learning
   c. self-reinforcement
   d. attributions for improvement

*5. The theoretical orientation held by marital and family therapists is
   a. psychoanalytic
   b. humanistic
   c. behavioral
   d. any of the above

6. In marital therapy, videotaping
   a. is rarely used, since it is too intimidating for couples who are already distressed.
   b. is used only during the assessment phase.
   c. is useful mainly for demonstrating techniques for the couple to try later at home.
   d. is useful for analyzing faulty patterns of communication.

7. How effective is family therapy in dealing with marital problems according to research?
   a. There is not sufficient research to establish it's effectiveness.
   b. It is effective primarily in saving marriages verging on divorce.
   c. It is effective primarily with well-established couples.
   d. It is effective with a wide range of marital problems.

8. Ms. K. opened up a YMCA in a poor community to provide free recreational resources to the children and adolescents. This is an example of
   a. primary prevention
   b. secondary prevention
   c. tertiary prevention
   d. none of the above

9. According to the text, suicide prevention centers
   a. are relatively ineffective as suicidal individuals are unlikely to call them.
   b. are much more effective if staffed by professionals rather than volunteers.
   c. are more helpful than friends in preventing suicide.
   d. should be continued despite lack of evidence of their effectiveness.

10. In practice, community mental health centers are
    a. very similar to traditional treatment programs.
    b. staffed by volunteers.
    c. focused exclusively on prevention.
    d. focused exclusively on inpatient services.

SHORT ANSWER

1. In _____ groups individuals learn and practice more effective ways of relating to other people.

2. Why is looking at levels of communication helpful to members of therapy groups?

3. Why is individualized behavior therapy conducted in groups?

4. Why has it been difficult to conduct research on the effectiveness of group therapy?

5. Why is conflict normal in marital and other long-term relationships?

6. Why might marital therapy concepts be applied to nonmarital problems?

7. describe the different services offered by community mental health centers (in five areas).

8. Describe a study that used community psychology methods to change harmful life styles.

9. What benefits can halfway houses and aftercare facilities provide according to research?

10. What are the advantages of using paraprofessionals in community mental health?

ANSWERS TO SELF-TEST, CHAPTER 20

MULTIPLE-CHOICE

1. B (p. 574)   2. B (p. 574)   3. B (p. 577-578)   4. B (p. 578)
5. D (p. 581)   6. D (p. 584-585) 7. D (p. 585-586)   8. A (p. 586)
9. D (p. 591)   10. A (p. 596)

SHORT ANSWER

1. Social-skills training (p. 577)

2. Normally we communicate on many levels so that what we intend to say (on one level) may not be what others receive (on another level). By looking at this group members become more aware of what they are communicating to (and receiving from) others. (p. 575-576)

3. Primarily for effeciency & economy although members probably also benefit from support/encouragement of others in group. (p. 576-577)

4. Group therapy is very complex with many variables, little agreement on how to measure success, etc. (p. 578-579º

5. Because there are so many areas in =which couples can agree or disagree. In addition the relationship keeps changing wich changes in jobs, children, etc. requiring repeated adjustments. (p. 581)

6. Even if the "problem" is not marital, marital therapy can help the couple cope with it and support each other.(p. 585)

7. Outpatient therapy (affordable, in the community), Short-term inpatient care, Day treatment, 24 hour emergency services, Consultation & education. (p.589-590)

8. Used mass media campaigns, educational groups, etc. to tell community how to reduce cardiovascular disease by changes in diet, smoking, exercise. (p. 593)

9. Enable patients to live & function in the community (not mental hospitals) thus reducing overall health care costs. (p. 593-594)

10. Clients can more easily identify with, work with. learn from, paraprofessionals from the same community & background. (p. 596)

21. Legal and Ethical Issues

OVERVIEW

The last three chapters dealt with various forms, techniques, or approaches to treatment. These included insight oriented therapies, behavioral therapies, and a variety of specialized approaches. This, the final chapter of the text, turns to legal and ethical issues in abnormal psychology.

CHAPTER SUMMARY

Psychologists struggle with many legal and ethical issues or dilemmas. Legal issues develop when an individual's mental condition becomes an issue in court. In *Criminal Commitment* cases, issues develop when individuals accused of crimes are found incompetent to stand trial or are acquitted by reason of insanity at the time of the crime. In *Civil Commitment* cases, individuals not accused of crimes may be committed to institutions if they are considered mentally ill and dangerous to themselves or others. It is not clear that either of these legal procedures are fair to the individuals involved or to larger society. Recent court rulings have clarified the legal rights of committed individuals, especially those civilly committed. These include rights to be treated in the least restrictive environment possible, to actually receive treatment, and to refuse treatment in some cases.

Ethical Issues in Therapy and Research cover a very broad area of individual rights. For example, psychologists recognize ethical obligations to obtain the informed consent of others before involving them in research and treatment. Yet research participants may behave differently if they completely understand what is being investigated and disturbed patients, under pressure from family and society, may not be able to choose freely or even to understand the consequences of their decisions. Therapists are also ethically and legally obligated to respect the confidentiality of their patients yet they may have to break confidentiality, for example, if their patients are endangering themselves or others. Such problems are very real ethical dilemmas that do not always have easy answers.

ESSENTIAL CONCEPTS

1. Criminal commitment apply to individuals suspected of being mentally ill and breaking laws while civil commitment procedures apply to individuals suspected of being mentally ill and dangerous.

2. The insanity defense deals with an individuals mental state at the time of a crime. Criteria of insanity continue to evolve and to be controversial.

3. Competency deals with an individuals mental state at the time of trial. It also raises difficult issues.

4. While the grounds for civil commitment vary from state to state, in virtually all states a person can be committed if they are (a) mentally ill and (b) unable to care for themselves or are a danger to self or others.

5. There is debate as to how accurately mental health professionals can predict the future dangerousness of a mentally disturbed individual.

6. Legal proceedings have addressed the rights of people committed through criminal and civil proceedings. These include being cared for in the least restrictive alternate setting, having the right to treatment not just minimal custodial care, and having the right to refuse particularly dangerous or noxious treatments.

7. Deinstitutionalization has been an effort to get committed people out of mental hospitals. Unfortunately it has led to other problems including homelessness.

8. Psychologists also face difficult ethical dilemmas in dealing with research participants and patients.

9. Regulations have been formulated to protect the rights of subjects in psychological research, such as the concept of informed consent -- informing the subject of the risks involved in the research and of their right to freely accept or reject participation in the experiment

10. The ethical codes of various mental health professions dictate that, with certain exceptions, the communication between patient and therapist must be kept confidential. Privileged communication laws extend this protection into the courts.

11. Therapists face additional ethical dilemmas in determining who is
    the client they are serving, what the goals for treatment should be,
    and what techniques should be used to achieve those goals.

KEY TERMS

Criminal commitment (p. 602)

Insanity (p. 603 & 609)

Competency to stand trial (p. 609)

Civil commitment (p. 611)

Informed consent (p. 623)

Confidentiality (p. 625)

Privileged communication (p. 625)

STUDY QUESTIONS

CRIMINAL COMMITMENT (p. 602)

1. What legal assumption underlies the insanity defense? Trace the history of the insanity defense using five landmark cases, guidelines and laws. What is the recent trend of decisions and why? (p. 602-606)

2. Read the case example (p. 606-607) and explain how it illustrates three additional problems with the concept of legal insanity. (p. 607-609)

3. Distinguish between "insanity" and "competency". What is the basic legal principle behind competency to stand trial? Compare competency to insanity in terms of (1) possible consequences and (2) clarity of guidelines. (p. 609-611)

CIVIL COMMITMENT (p. 611-621)

4. Identify the common criteria and types of civil commitment. (p. 611)

5. What is the legal dilemma in preventive detention of "dangerous" individuals?   Critique   traditional   research   on   predicting dangerousness.   Describe an alternative approach to this issue. (p. 611-613)

6. Summarize the recent trends in rates of involuntary commitment. Illustrate two reasons (one practical and one constitutional) that involuntary commitment remains an issue? (p. 613)

7. Summarize three recent trends protecting the rights of individuals who have been committed. How do ethical free will issues underlie these trends? How do Paul and Lentz propose to deal with these seemingly contradictory rights? (p. 614-618)

8. What factors led to deinstitutionalization policies? What were the unintended results? What future do Gralnick and others fear? (p. 618-621)

ETHICAL DILEMMAS IN THERAPY AND RESEARCH (p. 622-632)

9. Give two examples outside psychology that point to the need for ethical restraints in research. How are ethics codes and review panels used to protect research participants? (p. 622-623)

10. Summarize six ethical dilemmas being sure to point out why each is a dilemma (i.e. why it is not easily resolved). (p. 623-632)   Explain, especially, the distinction between confidentiality and privileged communication. (p. 625)

11. Summarize the textbook's concluding comments. (p. 632)

SELF-TEST, CHAPTER 21

MULTIPLE-CHOICE

1. What is the rationale of laws that provide for legal verdicts of "guilty but mentally ill"?
   a. to deal with mentally ill vagrants
   b. to permit consideration of whether the accused could appreciate the wrongfulness of his or her actions
   c. to provide treatment options for convicted criminals
   d. to prevent the truly insane from being treated as criminals

2. In the Jones v. United States case, the Supreme Court decided that a person could be considered dangerous
   a. only if they had previously committed a violent crime.
   b. if they are in a mental hospital & had previously committed crime.
   c. if they committed a crime that might have led to violence (even if not violent itself).
   d. only if the prosecutor proved beyond a reasonable doubt that they represent a danger to others.

3. Roger stole a watch from a store. His attorney proposed that Roger was incompetent to stand trial because of his mental condition (schizophrenia), and both the judge and prosecuting attorney agreed with this evaluation following testimony from several psychiatrists. What will happen to Roger?
   a. He will be found not guilty by reason of insanity and committed to a prison hospital until he is judged to be sane.
   b. He will be found not guilty by reason of insanity and committed to a prison hospital until he is judged to be no longer dangerous.
   c. He will be committed to a prison hospital, and his trial will be postponed until Roger is judged to be competent.
   d. He will be allowed to remain free in the community, but under observation, until he is judged to be competent.

4. Informal involuntary commitment to a mental hospital, without involvement of the courts,
   a. is prohibited in most states.
   b. can be instituted by a friend, relative, or police officer who is concerned about the person.
   c. can occur only on an emergency basis for a limited period of time.
   d. can occur if the person is judged by a psychiatrist to have a serious mental illness requiring treatment.

5. Monahan (1985) suggests that the prediction of violence is most accurate under the following conditions:
   a. in non-emergency situations
   b. when the person is currently in the hospital because of past dangerous behavior
   c. when a person can be evaluated over a period of time by a number of professionals in a controlled environment
   d. in an emergency, when violence appears imminent

*6. Donaldson, involuntarily committed to a psychiatric hospital for 14 years, sued the hospital psychiatrists, arguing that they had denied his right to
   a. refuse treatment.
   b. treatment.
   c. live in the least restrictive setting.
   d. medication.

7. Paul and Lentz (1977) propose that the decision of whether or not patients can refuse a particular treatment should be left to
   a. the patient.
   b. the parent or guardian.
   c. the court.
   d. an institutional review board.

8. Which of the following is not a concern voiced by Gralnick (1986) about the plight of the mentally ill in the years following deinstitutionalization?
   a. Seriously disturbed people will no longer be seen as mentally ill.
   b. Large numbers of mentally ill individuals will be returned to life in institutions, rather than treated on an outpatient basis.
   c. Mental illness will increasingly be seen as primarily biologically caused.
   d. Treatment of the mentally ill will focus too much on medication rather than psychotherapy.

9. Human subjects committees and institutional review boards for reviewing the ethics of proposed experiments are made up of
   a. behavioral scientists
   b. citizens of the community
   c. lawyers
   d. all of the above

10. The distinction between confidentiality and privileged
    communication is that only privileged communication legally
    protects individuals from
    a. being judged dangerous based on what they said.
    b. unethical practices of the therapist.
    c. being sued by the therapist for their statements.
    d. having what they said revealed in court.

SHORT ANSWER

1. Summarize the American Law Institute guidelines for defining
   criminal insanity.

2. What problems are faced by someone who succeeds in proving they
   are not guilty by reason of insanity (as shown by the illustration in
   the text)?

3. What is the difference between legal insanity and legal competency?

*4. What is the rationale or basis for Szasz's case against the use of
    the insanity defense?

5. On what basis may individuals be committed to a mental hospital
   against their will (civil commitment)?

6. Identify three legal protections or rights being extended to mental
   patients by recent legal decisions.

7. Identify two sources of ethical restraints on contemporary research.

8. Define "informed consent".

9. Give several reasons (text had 5) why therapists may reveal things clients tell them even when state law provides privileged communication for therapy relationships.

10. Are there circumstances where therapists are justified in inflicting pain on patients?

ANSWERS TO SELF-TEST, CHAPTER 21

MULTIPLE-CHOICE

1. C (p. 606)   2. C (p. 606-607)   3. C (p. 609-610)   4. C (p. 611)
5. D (p. 612)   6. B (p. 614-615)   7. D (p. 616-617)   8. B (p. 618-619)
9. D (p. 623)   10. D (p. 625)

SHORT ANSWER

1. A person is not responsible for criminal conduct if at the time of such conduct as a result of mental disease of defect he lacks substantial capacity either to appreciate the criminality (wrongfulness) of his conduct or to confirm his conduct to the requirements of law. (p. 604-605)

2. May be committed for longer period than they would have been imprisoned otherwise. May have difficulty proving they are no longer insane or dangerous. (p. 607-609)

3. Insanity deal with person's condition at the time of the crime Competency deals with condition at the time of trial. (p. 609)

4. That "being responsible" is a social judgment, not a personality characteristic. That even "different" people have the right to be treated like everyone else. (p. 608-609)

5. If they are mentally ill AND dangerous to themselves or others (which may include being unable to take care of themselves). (p. 611)

6. 1) right to least restrictive alternative for treatment, 2) right to receive treatment, 3) right to refuse treatment. (p. 614-616)

7. Ethical codes and guidelines, Committees to review ethics of proposed research. (p. 622)

8. Right to freely consent (or refuse) to participate in research after being informed of the procedure and any risks involved. (p. 623)

9. 1) Therapist judges client is dangerous, 2) Client introduces his/her sanity in a trial, 3) Client accuses therapist of malpractice, 4) Client is victim of child abuse (in some states), 5) Client initiated therapy to evade or plan a crime (in some states). (p. 625)

10. There is no clear answer to this. Perhaps brief aversive treatment could prevent long term disability or death. Careful consideration of ethical, legal, and psychological implications is needed. (p. 631-632)